I0517854

The Book On

Life Unscripted

What You Should Have Learned in High School

The Book On Series

By David Webb

Published by The Book On Publishing, 2025.

First edition. May 6, 2025.

Website: https://thebookon.ca

Substack: https://thebookonpublishing.substack.com/

LIFE UNSCRIPTED: What You Should Have Learned in High School

First edition. May 6, 2025.

Copyright © 2025 The Book On Publishing

ISBN: 978-1-997795-26-1

Written by David Webb.

The Book On Series

Dedication

To my incredible wife,
Robbin
Your unwavering support, love,
and belief in me, made this book possible.
This is for you.
David

Contents

Read This First

This is not a book designed to entertain you. It's not here to charm, to soothe, or to hold your hand. It won't dazzle you with stories, metaphors, or motivational fluff. What you're having is a tool, an instruction manual written for people who are serious about learning, executing, and thinking at a higher level.

Every book in The Book On series is built on a single premise: clarity beats complexity. We believe that when you strip away the noise, the emotions, the marketing spin, and the cultural rituals of "self-help," what's left is raw, unembellished instruction. That's what these books offer.

They are dry by design. Not because we don't care about language or narrative, but because when you're building something that matters, you don't need more distractions. You need a clear architecture. Mental scaffolding. Direction that respects your intelligence.

Each title in this series takes on a specific domain: decision-making, clarity, strategy, leverage, uncertainty, and drills deep, not in sweeping generalizations, but in applied frameworks. These are books for builders, operators, founders, tacticians, and thinkers—people who don't just consume knowledge but operationalize it.

You'll find no chapter-long anecdotes here. No self-congratulatory memoirs. No bullet-point platitudes. Instead, what you'll get is structured insight: argument, and the tone is direct. The prose is sober. The ideas are designed to be lifted out and used.

You won't be coddled, but you won't be misled either.

There's a place in the world for lyrical, emotional, story-driven books, and this isn't that place. This is a workspace. A blueprint. A conversation for people who are ready to act, not just absorb.

We respect your time and your intellect.

Welcome to The Book On series.

Section 1: Resilience and Adaptability

Introduction

Life presents challenges without warning. Career disruptions, relationship difficulties, financial pressures, and unexpected circumstances assess everyone. Your capacity to recover from setbacks and adjust to change decides much of your long-term stability and success.

Resilience is the ability to recover from adversity. Adaptability is the capacity to adjust to changing circumstances. These traits form the foundation of psychological strength and practical competence. Together, they enable you to face difficulties with confidence rather than panic.

This section provides comprehensive strategies for building both resilience and adaptability. Each chapter addresses a specific aspect of these capabilities, from managing emotions and reframing setbacks to building support networks and developing critical thinking skills. The methods presented here come from research in psychology and behavioral science, combined with practical observation of how people navigate difficult situations effectively.

By the end of this section, you will have concrete tools for managing stress, recovering from failure, keeping perspective during difficulties, and adapting to change. These are not abstract concepts. They are practical skills that strengthen with deliberate practice.

Chapter 1: Understanding Resilience and Adaptability

Resilience and adaptability are distinct but related capabilities. Understanding the difference helps you develop both systematically.

Resilience involves developing mental and emotional strength to cope with difficult situations. This includes managing unexpected changes, processing setbacks, and managing sustained stress. Resilient people do not avoid difficulties or remain unaffected by them. They experience the same emotional reactions as everyone else. The difference lies in their recovery process and their ability to keep function during adversity.

Building resilience requires several components. First, you need supportive relationships with people who provide emotional support and practical help. Second, you need effective self-care practices that keep your physical and mental health. Third, you need critical thinking skills that enable you to address challenges systematically rather than feeling overwhelmed by them.

These components are not mysterious. They are specific, learnable behaviors. Supportive relationships develop through consistent investment in connections with others. Self-care practices include adequate sleep, regular exercise, and stress management techniques. Critical thinking skills improve through deliberate practice in breaking down complex challenges into manageable steps.

Adaptability works differently. Where resilience helps you recover from adversity, adaptability helps you adjust to change. This might mean learning new skills when your field evolves, taking on unfamiliar roles when opportunities arise, or changing your approach when circumstances shift.

Adaptable people share several characteristics. They are still open to learning regardless of age or experience level. They take calculated risks rather than clinging to familiar but ineffective approaches. They accept that change is constant rather than viewing it as an aberration that should not occur.

Both resilience and adaptability develop through experience. You cannot build these capabilities purely through reading or contemplation. You must apply strategies in actual situations, see what works, and refine your approach based on results. This requires patience and sustained effort. There are no shortcuts.

Cultivating a Growth Mindset

A growth mindset is the understanding that abilities develop through effort rather than being fixed traits. This concept, developed by psychologist Carol Dweck, has substantial research support. People who believe they can improve through work actually do improve more than people who believe their capabilities are static.

When you adopt a growth mindset, setbacks become information rather than judgments. A failed attempt means your current approach needs adjustment, not that you lack fundamental capability. This distinction is crucial. If you interpret failure as evidence of fixed inadequacy, you stop trying. If you interpret it as feedback about your method, you adjust and continue.

Mistakes become valuable when viewed through a growth mindset. Each error reveals something about what does not work, which narrows the field of possible solutions. Successful people make many mistakes. The difference is they extract lessons from those mistakes rather than using them as evidence they should quit.

Challenges become opportunities rather than threats. When you meet something difficult, a fixed mindset triggers anxiety: what if I cannot do this? A growth mindset triggers curiosity: how can I learn to do this? This shift in perspective changes your emotional response and enables more productive problem-solving.

Embracing Challenges

Challenges force you to extend beyond comfortable patterns. Whether dealing with a difficult exam, navigating an uncomfortable conversation, or managing new responsibilities, these situations push you to develop capabilities you did not previously have.

Growth occurs outside familiar territory. When everything is comfortable and easy, you are not developing new capabilities. You are keeping existing ones. This is necessary for some activities, but sustained growth requires regular exposure to challenges that exceed your current capacity.

Challenges push you to think differently, get new skills, and develop creative solutions. They teach you to keep composure under pressure and adapt to unfamiliar situations. Over time, this process reduces anxiety around uncertainty and builds genuine confidence based on proven capability.

The key is reframing challenges from threats to problems worth solving. This cognitive shift changes your emotional response. Threats trigger avoidance and anxiety. Problems trigger engagement and creative thinking. The situation has not changed. Your interpretation of it has, which completely alters your response.

When facing a significant challenge, break it into manageable components. Large problems feel overwhelming because your mind cannot process all the variables simultaneously. Finding smaller, discrete tasks makes the work tractable. Each completed task provides momentum and clarifies the next step. This is not avoiding the challenge. It is approaching it systematically.

Developing Problem-Solving Approaches

When problems arise, shift immediately into problem-solving mode. This does not mean suppressing emotional responses. It means not letting emotional responses dominate your decision-making. Acknowledge difficulty and frustration. Then ask: what can I control? What information do I need? What is the next smallest action I can take?

This structured approach prevents the paralysis that often goes with major challenges. You may not know how to solve the entire problem. But you can usually find one small action that moves toward a solution. Take that action. Reassess. Find the next small action. This iterative process builds momentum and often reveals solutions that were not clear initially.

Self-Compassion and Progress Tracking

Self-compassion means treating yourself with the same patience you would extend to someone you care about who is learning something difficult. This is not about lowering standards or excusing poor performance. It is about keeping perspective when you make mistakes.

Everyone makes errors while learning. Everyone experiences setbacks. Treating these moments as catastrophic failures undermines confidence and motivation. Treating them as normal parts of the learning process supports forward momentum. The difference in outcomes is huge.

Track your progress deliberately. Small wins accumulate but often go unnoticed without conscious attention. Getting started on a task you were avoiding is progress. Sending a difficult email is progress. Managing a full day of responsibilities without falling apart is progress. Each step forward builds confidence and shows capability.

Ongoing Development

Building resilience and adaptability is continuous work, not a one-time achievement. These capabilities develop and strengthen throughout life. As you meet new challenges and navigate unexpected changes, these skills become more refined and dependable.

Each time you face a setback, navigate change, or push yourself beyond your comfort zone, you strengthen your ability to manage stress, solve problems, and keep equilibrium. The strategies presented in this chapter are not temporary techniques. They are lifelong practices that serve you across all contexts.

Chapter 2: Reframing Failure

Failure triggers disappointment, frustration, and often shame. These reactions are normal. They are also obstacles to learning. The emotional weight of failure often prevents people from extracting the valuable information failures provide.

Despite its emotional impact, failure is both inevitable and necessary for growth. No one achieves lasting success without meeting large setbacks. Examining the careers of accomplished people in any field reveals consistent patterns: early failures, persistent effort despite those failures, and eventual success built on lessons learned through earlier attempts.

The difference between people who thrive and people who stagnate is not the presence or absence of failure. It is how they respond to it. Learning to view failure as information rather than judgment enables you to develop greater resilience, adaptability, and long-term effectiveness.

Understanding Failure as Feedback

Failure is not an endpoint. It is a signal that something needs adjustment. This reframing is not semantic manipulation. It is correct description of what failure is. When an approach fails, you have learned that particular method does not work in that context. This is valuable information.

By viewing failure as a natural part of the learning process, you reduce anxiety, self-doubt, and avoidance behaviors. Instead of withdrawing when things go wrong, you are still engaged and adjust your approach.

This persistence, guided by lessons from earlier attempts, is what produces eventual success.

Reframing failure builds resilience by shifting focus from defeat to development. It strengthens problem-solving abilities, improves judgment, and provides the confidence to take calculated risks. All of these capabilities are essential for achieving meaningful goals.

Reframing does not mean ignoring disappointment. It means acknowledging setbacks without allowing them to define your identity or capabilities. By extracting lessons from mistakes, you build resilience, develop critical thinking skills, and strengthen your capacity to manage future challenges.

Analyzing Setbacks Systematically

When something goes wrong, analyze it systematically rather than emotionally. Ask specific questions: What aspects of my approach worked? What aspects did not work? What factors contributed to the outcome? What information was I missing? What could I do differently?

This analysis should be thorough but not obsessive. The goal is to extract actionable insights, not to ruminate endlessly on every detail. Find the one or two most significant factors that influenced the outcome. Focus on elements within your control or influence. Accept factors outside your control without dwelling on them.

Document your analysis. Writing clarifies thinking. When you force yourself to articulate what went wrong and what you learned, patterns become visible that remain obscure in purely mental review. These written records also prevent repeating the same mistakes later when memory has faded.

Focusing on Effort and Progress

Focus on effort and progress rather than only on results. Results matter. They provide necessary feedback about whether your approach is working. However, results are single data points. Effort and progress represent trajectory.

Every attempt, every practice session, every incremental improvement contributes to eventual success even when individual results disappoint. Consistent effort compounds over time. This compounding effect is not at once visible, which is why many people abandon effective approaches prematurely. They judge their method based on short-term results before the cumulative effect of sustained effort becomes clear.

When evaluating your progress, consider whether you are making better attempts, not just whether you are achieving better results. Better attempts eventually produce better results, but there is often a delay. Understanding this delay prevents premature abandonment of approaches that would work with continued effort.

Redefining Success

If success required perfection, few people would achieve anything meaningful. Redefining success means letting go of the expectation that you must execute everything flawlessly. Very few complex skills work this way. Mastery develops through accumulated imperfect attempts, not through waiting until you can perform perfectly.

When you shift from demanding perfection to prioritizing growth, learning becomes more sustainable and considerably less stressful. Attempting something new no longer feels like a test with one correct answer. It becomes an exploration with multiple paths forward and valuable lessons available regardless of immediate outcome.

This shift also makes you more willing to take on ambitious challenges. Fear of failure paralyzes when failure means personal inadequacy. When failure means information about your current approach, trying difficult things becomes rational rather than threatening.

Building Forward from Setbacks

After a setback, find specifically what went wrong. General feelings of failure are not useful. They provide no direction for improvement. Specific identification of problems enables specific solutions.

Once you understand what failed, figure out what you need to improve. This might mean developing other skills, seeking guidance from someone with relevant experience, gathering more information before continuing, or evaluating your approach on a smaller scale before full implementation. Find the specific gap and create a plan to address it.

Every significant achievement builds on a foundation of failed attempts. The only difference between people who succeed and people who do not is that successful people continue adjusting their approach after failures rather than stopping. This persistence, informed by lessons from earlier attempts, is what produces eventual success.

Separating Failure from Identity

Failing at something does not make you a failure. This distinction is crucial. One of the most damaging cognitive patterns is conflating a specific failure with your overall competence or worth as a person.

A failed business venture means that particular business did not work. It does not mean you lack business capability. A rejected job application means you did not get that particular position. It does not mean you are unemployable. A failed relationship means that relationship did not work. It does not mean you are incapable of successful relationships.

Instead of catastrophizing failure, recognize it as an event with specific causes, not a judgment of your fundamental worth or capability. Remind yourself that trying something difficult is evidence of effort and engagement, not evidence of inadequacy. Most people avoid trying things where failure is possible. By trying, you show more courage than those who never try.

Mistakes show you are learning. This is not consolation. It is fact. Learning necessarily involves errors. If you are not making mistakes, you are not challenging yourself sufficiently to produce growth. The absence of failure signals the absence of meaningful challenge.

The Road Ahead

Everyone faces setbacks in relationships, careers, education, and personal development. The setback itself matters less than your response to it. By adopting the strategies presented in this chapter, you develop the courage to embrace challenges, the wisdom to learn from mistakes, and the resilience to convert failure into progress. These capabilities distinguish people who achieve meaningful goals from people who stay trapped by fear of failure.

Chapter 3: Strengthening Emotional Regulation

Emotions drive motivation, strengthen relationships, and inspire action toward goals. When emotions become overwhelming, whether anxiety, frustration, or stress, they can cloud judgment and impair effective response. This is where emotional regulation becomes essential.

Emotional regulation is not suppression. It is the ability to experience emotions, understand what triggers them, and respond in ways that serve your goals rather than undermine them. This capability develops through practice and specific techniques.

At the core of emotional regulation is mindfulness: training attention to remain grounded in the present moment. By developing mindfulness, you learn to see emotions without being controlled by them. This enables thoughtful response rather than impulsive reaction.

This chapter explores practical techniques for strengthening emotional regulation, including meditation practices, breathing exercises, and progressive muscle relaxation. These methods help support calm, clarity, and emotional balance even in difficult situations.

Understanding Emotional Regulation

Emotional regulation is the ability to manage emotional responses in ways that serve your wellbeing and goals. This involves several components: recognizing emotions as they arise, understanding what triggers them, tolerating uncomfortable emotions without acting impulsively, and choosing responses aligned with your values.

Poor emotional regulation manifests in various ways. You might lash out when frustrated, withdraw when anxious, or make impulsive decisions to escape discomfort. These reactions often create more problems beyond the original difficulty. Strong emotional regulation allows you to experience emotions without being controlled by them.

Developing emotional regulation does not mean becoming emotionless or suppressing feelings. Emotional suppression is counterproductive. It increases psychological distress and often leads to more intense emotional eruptions later. Effective emotional regulation means acknowledging feelings, understanding their source, and choosing constructive responses.

The Role of Mindfulness

Mindfulness is sustained attention to the present moment without judgment. This practice forms the foundation of emotional regulation. When you practice mindfulness, you see your thoughts and feelings as they occur without immediately reacting to them or categorizing them as good or bad.

Mindfulness activates the relaxation response, the physiological opposite of the stress response. Regular practice lowers cortisol levels, reduces blood pressure, improves sleep quality, and enhances cognitive function. These are not subjective feelings. They are measurable physiological changes.

The practice is straightforward but not easy. You focus attention on a chosen object: your breath, physical sensations, or sounds in your environment. When attention wanders, and it will constantly, you notice this without judgment and gently redirect focus. This simple practice, repeated consistently, builds significant mental capacity over time.

Mindfulness does not drop stress or difficult emotions. It changes your relationship with them. Instead of being swept away by emotional reactions, you develop the capacity to see them with some distance. This space between stimulus and response is where choice exists.

Meditation Practices

Meditation trains attention and awareness. Various forms exist, but all share the goal of developing mental clarity and emotional stability through focused attention practice.

Mindfulness meditation is the most accessible form for beginners. Sit comfortably with your spine straight. Close your eyes or lower your gaze. Focus attention on your breath, noticing the sensation of air entering and leaving your body. When your mind wanders, acknowledge this without self-criticism and return attention to your breath. Start with five minutes daily and gradually increase duration.

Body scan meditation systematically directs attention through different parts of your body. Start at your feet. Notice any sensations: temperature, pressure, tension, or relaxation. Move gradually upward through your legs, torso, arms, and head. This practice develops awareness of how emotions manifest physically. Anxiety might appear as chest tightness. Stress might show as shoulder tension. Recognizing these patterns helps you address emotions before they become overwhelming.

Loving-kindness meditation cultivates compassion toward yourself and others. Begin by directing well-wishes toward yourself: may I be happy, may I be healthy, may I be safe. Then extend these wishes to someone you care about, to neutral parties, to difficult people in your life, and eventually to all beings. This practice reduces stress caused by interpersonal conflict and builds emotional resilience.

Consistency matters more than duration. Five minutes of daily practice produces better results than one hour practiced sporadically. The goal is building a habit, not achieving perfect concentration. You will never achieve perfect concentration. The practice is in noticing when attention has drifted and bringing it back.

Deep Breathing Techniques

Deep breathing directly influences the autonomic nervous system. Slow, deep breathing activates the parasympathetic nervous system, which promotes relaxation and reduces the physiological stress response. This is not metaphorical. Breathing directly alters your body chemistry and neural activity.

Diaphragmatic breathing involves breathing deeply into your abdomen rather than shallowly into your chest. Place one hand on your chest and one on your abdomen. When you inhale, your abdomen should expand while your chest stays relatively still. This ensures you use your full lung capacity. Practice this for a few minutes several times daily until it becomes natural.

The four-seven-eight technique is particularly effective for managing acute stress or preparing for sleep. Inhale through your nose for four counts. Hold your breath for seven counts. Exhale completely through your mouth for eight counts. The extended exhale activates the relaxation response. Repeat this cycle three to four times.

Box breathing creates a rhythmic pattern that focuses attention and reduces anxiety. Inhale for four counts. Hold for four counts. Exhale for four counts. Hold empty for four counts. Repeat. This technique is used by military personnel and first responders to keep composure in high-stress situations.

These techniques work anywhere, anytime, without special equipment or preparation. Use them before stressful events, during difficult conversations, or whenever you notice anxiety rising. They provide immediate physiological intervention in stress response.

Progressive Muscle Relaxation

Progressive muscle relaxation systematically tenses and releases different muscle groups throughout your body. This practice helps you recognize the difference between tension and relaxation and teaches you to release physical stress you may not realize you are carrying.

Start with your feet. Tense the muscles in your feet for five seconds, creating noticeable tension but not pain. Then release completely and notice the sensation of relaxation for ten to fifteen seconds. Move systematically upward through your calves, thighs, buttocks, abdomen, chest, hands, arms, shoulders, neck, and face.

This technique is particularly useful before sleep or after prolonged periods of concentration. It helps discharge accumulated physical tension and creates a state of physical calm that supports mental calm. Many people carry chronic tension without awareness. Progressive muscle relaxation builds consciousness of this tension and provides a method for releasing it.

Building a Practice

Start small. Choose one technique and practice it for five to ten minutes daily for two weeks. Once this becomes habitual, you can expand your practice or explore other techniques. The goal is consistent practice, not perfect execution.

Use these techniques preventatively, not just during crises. Regular practice builds baseline resilience that makes you more capable of handling stress when it arises. Trying to learn these skills in the middle of a crisis is far less effective than having practiced them regularly beforehand.

Track your practice and notice changes. Do you sleep better? Do you recover from stress more quickly? Do you find it easier to focus? These changes often occur gradually, but they accumulate significantly over time. Many people abandon these practices because immediate dramatic effects do not appear. The benefits are real but develop progressively.

The Road Ahead

Emotional regulation is a learnable skill that improves quality of life substantially. Through mindfulness, meditation, breathing techniques, and progressive muscle relaxation, you develop the capacity to remain calm under pressure, make clear-headed decisions, and support wellbeing even when external circumstances are difficult. These are not personality traits you either have or lack. They are capabilities that strengthen with consistent practice.

Chapter 4: Developing Cognitive Reframing Skills

Your thoughts shape your interpretation of events and your emotional responses to them. When facing challenges or uncertainty, negative thought patterns can intensify stress and undermine effective coping. Cognitive reframing is a mental strategy that helps you challenge these patterns and develop more constructive perspectives.

Cognitive reframing is not positive thinking or self-deception. It is the systematic examination of your interpretations and assumptions to find distortions and develop more exact, helpful perspectives. This process comes from cognitive behavioral therapy, which has substantial evidence supporting its effectiveness.

This chapter provides practical tools for finding negative thought patterns, challenging limiting beliefs, and adopting healthier thinking habits. These skills enable you to respond to difficulties with greater clarity and resilience.

Understanding Cognitive Distortions

Cognitive distortions are systematic errors in thinking that negatively affect how you interpret events.

Everyone engages in these patterns occasionally. The problem arises when they become habitual and unconscious, consistently distorting your sense of reality.

Common cognitive distortions include all-or-nothing thinking, where you see situations in absolute terms without recognizing middle ground. For example, viewing yourself as either completely successful or a total failure, with no recognition of partial success or progress. This pattern creates unrealistic standards and frequent disappointment.

Overgeneralization involves drawing broad conclusions from limited evidence. One rejection becomes proof that you will always be rejected. One mistake becomes evidence that you cannot do anything right. This pattern amplifies the significance of negative events while ignoring contradictory evidence.

Catastrophizing involves assuming the worst possible outcome will occur. A headache becomes a brain tumor. An unanswered text means the relationship is over. This pattern generates excessive anxiety about unlikely scenarios while preventing realistic assessment of actual risk.

Mind reading assumes you know what others think without evidence. You interpret neutral actions as negative judgments. This pattern damages relationships and creates anxiety about social interactions based on assumptions rather than reality.

Should statements impose rigid rules about how you or others must behave. When reality does not meet these expectations, you experience frustration, guilt, or resentment. These statements often reflect internalized standards that may not serve you well.

Recognizing these patterns in your own thinking is the first step toward changing them. Most people engage in these distortions automatically without awareness. Building awareness requires deliberate attention to your thoughts, particularly during times of stress or difficulty.

Identifying Your Thought Patterns

Start by noticing your automatic thoughts during emotionally charged situations. When you feel strong emotions, pause and name what thoughts preceded that feeling. Write these thoughts down. This external record helps you examine them more objectively than you can through pure introspection.

Track patterns over time. Do certain types of situations consistently trigger specific thought patterns? Do you catastrophize about health concerns? Do you engage in all-or-nothing thinking about performance? Finding your particular patterns enables targeted intervention.

Notice the language you use in self-talk. Words like always, never, should, and must often signal cognitive distortions. Absolute language rarely reflects reality accurately. Life exists in shades of gray, not absolute categories.

Challenging Distorted Thoughts

Once you find distorted thinking, challenge it systematically. Ask: What evidence supports this thought? What evidence contradicts it? Am I making assumptions without facts? Am I catastrophizing or overgeneralizing? What would I tell a friend thinking this way?

Examine the evidence objectively. Cognitive distortions feel true because they generate strong emotions. Emotions are not evidence. Separate feeling from fact. Just because something feels catastrophic does not make it actually catastrophic. Just because you feel like a failure does not make you actually a failure.

Consider alternative explanations. If someone does not return your call, cognitive distortions might suggest they are angry or no longer care about you. Alternative explanations might include: they are busy, they did not see the call, they plan to respond later, or their phone died. Most situations have multiple possible interpretations. Jumping to negative conclusion without evidence creates unnecessary distress.

Evaluate your predictions. If you predict catastrophe, explicitly note this prediction and later assess whether it occurred. Most catastrophic predictions do not materialize. Building awareness of this pattern helps you recognize catastrophizing in future situations and respond with proper skepticism toward these predictions.

Reframing Negative Thoughts

Reframing involves developing more balanced, correct perspectives. This is not replacing negative thoughts with unrealistic positive thoughts. It is replacing distorted thoughts with realistic ones.

For all-or-nothing thinking, find the middle ground. Instead of "I am either completely successful or a total failure," recognize that "I achieved some goals and fell short on others. This is normal and provides direction for improvement."

For overgeneralization, add specificity. Instead of "I always mess things up," recognize that "I made a mistake in this specific situation. I have also succeeded in many situations. This one error does not define my overall capability."

For catastrophizing, assess realistic probability and consequences. Instead of "This headache might be a brain tumor," recognize that "Most headaches have benign causes. If this persists or worsens, I will consult a doctor. Worrying about unlikely scenarios does not help."

For mind reading, acknowledge uncertainty. Instead of "They think I am incompetent," recognize that "I do not actually know what they think. Their neutral expression does not necessarily show negative judgment. I can ask for feedback rather than assuming."

For should statements, examine whether your standards are realistic and helpful. Instead of "I should never make mistakes," recognize that "Making mistakes is part of learning. Perfection is impossible. I can aim for continuous improvement rather than flawlessness."

Building New Thought Patterns

Changing thought patterns requires consistent practice. Cognitive distortions develop over years and do not disappear after one correction. Each time you notice a distortion and reframe it, you strengthen neural pathways supporting more balanced thinking. Over time, more realistic thinking becomes more automatic.

Practice gratitude deliberately. This is not about forced positivity. It is about directing attention toward what is working in addition to what is not. Spend a few minutes daily noting things you appreciate. This practice counterbalances the natural tendency to focus disproportionately on problems and difficulties.

Develop self-compassionate self-talk. Notice how you speak to yourself during difficulties. Would you speak to someone you care about in the same way? If not, consciously adopt more compassionate language. This is not about lowering standards. It is about keeping perspective and encouragement rather than harsh self-criticism that undermines motivation.

Challenge perfectionism systematically. Perfectionism is not high standards. High standards are motivating and achievable. Perfectionism is the belief that anything less than perfect is failure. This belief generates anxiety, procrastination, and chronic dissatisfaction. Replace perfectionist standards with excellence-oriented standards: doing your best while accepting that mistakes and limitations are inevitable.

Using Cognitive Reframing During Stress

Cognitive reframing is particularly valuable during stressful situations when emotional reactions are strong. In these moments, your thoughts strongly influence whether stress becomes manageable or overwhelming.

When facing a stressor, pause and name your automatic thoughts about it. Are you catastrophizing?

Are you overgeneralizing? Challenge these thoughts explicitly. What is the actual worst-case scenario versus the one you are imagining? What are more likely outcomes? What resources do you have for handling this?

Reframe stressors as challenges rather than threats when possible. Threats suggest danger and trigger defensive reactions. Challenges suggest opportunities to show capability and trigger engaged problem-solving. This shift in framing changes your physiological and psychological response.

Focus on what you can control. Cognitive distortions often fixate on factors outside your control, which generates helplessness and anxiety. Deliberately redirect attention to aspects within your control or influence. You may not control outcomes, but you usually control your effort, preparation, and response.

The Road Ahead

Cognitive reframing is a powerful tool for building resilience and managing stress. By finding cognitive distortions, challenging distorted thoughts, and developing more balanced perspectives, you reduce unnecessary emotional distress and respond to difficulties more effectively. These skills require consistent practice but produce substantial improvements in emotional wellbeing and life satisfaction. Your thoughts are not facts. They are interpretations, and interpretations can be examined and revised.

Chapter 5: Building Strong Support

Support networks are fundamental to resilience and sustained performance. Research consistently shows that individuals with strong social connections experience better mental health outcomes, more effective stress management, and greater success in achieving personal and professional goals. The quality of your relationships directly affects your capacity to manage challenges, recover from setbacks, and keep perspective during difficult periods.

A support network is not simply a collection of contacts or acquaintances. It consists of meaningful relationships with people who provide emotional support, practical aid, and honest feedback. These relationships function as both safety net and accelerant: they cushion you during difficulties while also propelling you toward your goals. Understanding how to build and support these connections deliberately is a critical life skill.

The Function of Social Support

Social support works through several distinct mechanisms. Emotional support provides validation, empathy, and reassurance during stressful situations. When you face uncertainty or difficulty, having someone who listens without judgment and acknowledges your experience reduces psychological distress and helps you process emotions effectively. This type of support is particularly valuable during personal crises, major life transitions, or periods of sustained stress.

Informational support involves guidance, advice, and knowledge sharing. This might include a mentor explaining how to navigate a complex situation, a colleague sharing expertise about an unfamiliar process, or a friend who has successfully managed a similar challenge offering perspective. Informational support helps you make better decisions by expanding your understanding of available options and potential consequences.

Instrumental support refers to tangible help: someone helping you move, proofreading an important document, providing a professional introduction, or lending equipment you need. While this practical help is obviously useful, it also signals that people are willing to invest time and effort in your success, which has psychological benefits beyond the immediate help.

Companionship and belonging represent another crucial dimension. Regular positive interaction with people who share your values and interests provides a sense of connection that counters isolation. This matters for mental health regardless of whether you are facing specific problems. Humans are social animals; sustained isolation produces measurable negative effects on both physical and psychological wellbeing.

Evidence for Social Support Benefits

Research across multiple disciplines confirms the importance of social connections. Studies in health psychology show that people with strong social networks recover more quickly from illness, experience less severe symptoms during illness, and keep better overall health. The effect size is substantial: some research suggests that weak social connections carry health risks comparable to smoking or obesity.

In occupational contexts, social support predicts job satisfaction, performance, and career advancement. Employees with supportive colleagues and mentors report lower burnout rates, greater engagement, and more successful navigation of workplace challenges. Networking quality, not just quantity, correlates with salary increases and promotion rates.

During major life transitions—such as starting college, entering the workforce, moving, or experiencing relationship changes—social support buffers against the stress inherent in these changes. People with strong support networks adapt more successfully to new circumstances and keep better mental health during adjustment periods.

Building Supportive Relationships Deliberately

Effective support networks do not typically develop by accident. They require intentional cultivation. The first step is finding what types of support you currently have and what gaps exist. Some people have abundant emotional support but lack professional mentorship. Others may have extensive professional networks but few relationships where they can be vulnerable about personal struggles. Honest assessment of your current network helps you find where to invest energy.

Seek relationships with diverse people who can provide different types of support. A well-rounded network includes peers who understand your current circumstances, mentors who have navigated paths you aspire to follow, and friends who know you well enough to provide honest feedback. Diversity in perspectives, experiences, and areas of expertise strengthens your network's overall utility.

Proximity and regular interaction matter significantly. You build stronger relationships with people you interact with often. This explains why coworkers often become friends and why maintaining long-distance friendships requires deliberate effort. When possible, invest in relationships with people you meet regularly through work, education, community activities, or shared interests. These relationships develop more naturally through consistent interaction.

Join groups or communities aligned with your interests and values. Whether professional associations, athletic teams, volunteer organizations, religious communities, or hobby groups, these contexts offer natural opportunities to meet people with shared interests. Shared activities give you concrete things to discuss and do together, which eases relationship development.

Be strategic about where you invest time. Not every acquaintance needs to become a close friend, and not every friendly interaction needs to develop into a lasting relationship. Focus your energy on relationships that feel mutually beneficial and where you genuinely enjoy the other person's company. Quality matters far more than quantity.

Quality Over Quantity in Relationships

Research on social relationships consistently finds that a few close, high-quality relationships provide more benefit than many superficial connections. Anthropologist Robin Dunbar's work suggests that humans can support approximately five close relationships, fifteen good friends, fifty casual friends, and 150 acquaintances at any given time. These numbers vary somewhat by individual, but the principle holds: you have limited capacity for deep relationships.

A high-quality relationship is characterized by reciprocity, trust, and genuine care. Both parties invest in the relationship, provide support when needed, and feel comfortable being authentic. You can discuss both successes and struggles. The relationship enriches both people's lives rather than depleting either person.

Low-quality relationships drain more than they provide. These might be relationships where you feel you must constantly prove yourself, where support flows only one direction, where you cannot be honest about your thoughts or feelings, or where interaction consistently leaves you feeling worse. Some relationships are actively toxic, involving manipulation, consistent criticism, or exploitation. Being selective about which relationships you support is not selfishness; it is necessary self-preservation.

Evaluate relationships honestly. If a relationship consistently causes stress, requires you to compromise your values, or involves someone who is unreliable or dismissive of your needs, that relationship is not serving you well. You can reduce investment in such relationships or end them entirely. This is particularly important when resources are limited: time and emotional energy you spend on draining relationships are resources unavailable for healthy relationships.

Maintaining Connections Over Time

Relationships require ongoing maintenance. Even strong friendships can fade without regular contact and mutual investment. As life circumstances change—graduation, new jobs, relocations, relationship changes, supporting connections requires more deliberate effort.

Schedule regular contact with important relationships. This might mean a weekly phone call, monthly meetup, or regular video chat for long-distance friends. Treating these connections as priorities worthy of calendar space signals their importance and ensures you keep them despite competing demands.

Stay informed about what matters to people in your network. Remember significant events in their lives, ask follow-up questions about ongoing situations they have mentioned, and acknowledge milestones and accomplishments. This shows that you value them as individuals, not just as sources of support for yourself.

Be dependable. Show up when you commit to meeting someone. Follow through on promises. Respond to messages within a reasonable timeframe. If you cannot provide help someone has asked, be honest about that rather than agreeing and not delivering. Reliability builds trust, which is the foundation of strong relationships.

Reciprocate support. Pay attention to when people in your network need help and offer it proactively. Strong relationships involve mutual support, not one-directional help. If you only reach out when you need something, relationships weaken over time.

Accept that some relationships will naturally fade. As circumstances change, some connections that once were central become less relevant to your current life. This is normal. You cannot keep all relationships with equal intensity indefinitely. Focus energy on relationships that stay mutually beneficial rather than trying to preserve connections that no longer serve either party well.

Asking for Help Effectively

Many people struggle to ask for help, viewing it as weakness or imposition. This perspective is counterproductive. Asking for help when you need it is a skill, not a failing. People generally want to help others, and most individuals feel pleased when asked for help in areas where they have expertise or resources.

Be specific about what you need. Rather than saying "I need help with my job search," request particular help: "Could you review my resume?" or "Would you be willing to introduce me to someone who works in that field?" Specific requests are easier to fulfill and make it clear what would actually be useful.

Respect people's time and boundaries. When asking for help, acknowledge that you understand the person may not be able to help. Provide enough context that they can make an informed decision about whether and how to help. If someone declines or offers less than you asked, accept this gracefully. People have limits on their available time and energy.

Time your requests appropriately. Do not ask for significant help during periods when someone is obviously overwhelmed with their own challenges. Be aware of what is happening in people's lives and adjust your requests accordingly.

Express genuine gratitude when people help you. Acknowledge the specific ways their help had an influence. This reinforces the relationship and makes the person more likely to help again in the future. Follow up later to let them know how things turned out. Closing the loop shows that you valued their contribution.

Build relationships before you need them. If you only reach out when you need something, people will notice. Regular positive interaction creates the foundation of reciprocity that makes asking for help feel natural rather than extractive.

Recognizing Unhealthy Relationship Patterns

Not all relationships contribute positively to your life. Some relationships are actively harmful. Recognizing unhealthy patterns allows you to make informed decisions about which relationships to keep, change, or end.

Consistently one-sided relationships create resentment and drain your resources. If you are always the one starting contact, providing support, making compromises, or investing effort while the other person contributes minimally, this imbalance is unsustainable. Healthy relationships involve reciprocal investment from both parties.

Relationships that require you to constantly prove your worth or walk on eggshells are psychologically exhausting. If you feel anxious about how someone will react to normal requests or expressions of your needs, if you must carefully manage your behavior to avoid criticism or conflict, or if you feel your needs are consistently dismissed, this dynamic is harmful.

Manipulation and exploitation are serious red flags. This includes people who use guilt to control your behavior, who consistently violate boundaries you have set up, who take credit for your work or ideas, or who share your confidences with others despite your request for privacy. These behaviors show a fundamental lack of respect.

Consistent criticism or undermining disguised as concern is toxic. Someone who regularly points out your flaws, dismisses your accomplishments, or suggests you are incapable of managing your own decisions is not supportive, regardless of how they frame their behavior. Genuine support involves constructive feedback when requested and encouragement of your growth, not constant diminishment.

Social isolation tactics are warning signs of potentially abusive relationships. If someone consistently discourages your connections with other people, creates conflict between you and your other friends or family, or demands all your time and attention, this is concerning. Healthy relationships encourage you to keep a varied support network, not to depend entirely on one person.

Trust your feelings about relationships. If interactions consistently leave you feeling anxious, diminished, guilty, or exhausted rather than energized or supported, pay attention to that pattern. While all relationships involve occasional difficulty or conflict, the overall trajectory should be positive for both parties.

Addressing Relationship Difficulties

Most relationships meet problems at some point. The question is whether issues can be addressed constructively or show fundamental incompatibility.

Direct communication often resolves misunderstandings and minor conflicts. If someone's behavior bothers you, consider whether they may be unaware of the impact. Clearly explaining how specific behaviors affect you, without attacking the person's character, often leads to positive changes. For example, "When you cancel plans at the last minute, I feel disrespected because I have turned down other opportunities to spend time with you" is more productive than "You are always flaky and unreliable."

Be willing to hear feedback about your own behavior. If someone tells you that your actions have hurt them, listen without becoming defensive. Consider whether their perspective has validity. Be willing to change behaviors that negatively affect people you care about.

Establish and keep clear boundaries. You have the right to decide what behaviors you will and will not accept in relationships. Communicate these boundaries directly. If someone repeatedly violates boundaries after you have clearly said them, this shows disrespect. You must then decide whether to accept this dynamic or reduce your investment in that relationship.

Some relationship problems cannot be fixed through communication. If someone is fundamentally incompatible with your values, if they are dealing with issues they are unwilling to address, or if the relationship dynamic is inherently unhealthy, ending or significantly reducing the relationship may be the proper choice. This is not failure; it is recognizing that not all relationships should be kept indefinitely.

Adapting Your Network to Life Changes

Your support needs change as your life circumstances change. The network that served you well during high school may not meet your needs in college or early career. Recognizing this and adapting accordingly is important.

Major transitions often require developing new relationships while keeping important existing ones. Starting college, you need to build new friendships with people in your current environment while staying connected with high school friends who are still important. Beginning your career, you need professional mentors and workplace relationships while keeping personal friendships.

Seek out people who understand your current situation. While long-term friends who have known you for years provide valuable continuity, relationships with people navigating similar current challenges offer specific relevant support. Both types of relationships serve important functions.

Be proactive about finding what support you need as circumstances change. If you are starting a new job, you need colleagues who can explain organizational culture and unwritten rules. If you are dealing with a health issue, you may receive help from connecting with others who have faced similar challenges. If you are developing a new skill, you need mentors with ability in that area. Deliberately seek relationships that meet emerging needs rather than assuming your existing network can address all situations.

The Road Ahead

Building and supporting strong support networks is an ongoing process requiring intentionality and effort. The relationships you develop serve as foundation for resilience, providing both emotional support and practical help throughout your life. These connections help you navigate challenges, achieve goals, and support wellbeing.

Invest in relationships deliberately. Seek connections with people who enhance your life while contributing positively to theirs. Maintain regular contact with important relationships. Reciprocate support generously. Ask for help when you need it. Address problems directly and honestly. End or reduce relationships that consistently diminish rather than support you.

Remember that quality matters far more than quantity. A few deep, reciprocal relationships provide more value than many superficial connections. Focus your energy accordingly. The effort you invest in building and maintaining supportive relationships is among the most valuable investments you can make.

Chapter 6: Develop Critical Thinking Skills

Problem-solving ability is perhaps the most transferable skill you can develop. Whether dealing with academic challenges, workplace obstacles, interpersonal conflicts, financial constraints, or personal decisions, the capacity to systematically analyze situations and find effective solutions decides your success across virtually all life domains.

Many people approach problems reactively, responding emotionally or implementing the first solution that occurs to them. This often leads to suboptimal outcomes and creates added problems. Developing a structured approach to problem-solving improves decision quality, reduces stress, and builds confidence in your ability to manage challenges.

Understanding the Nature of Problems

Problems exist when current reality differs from desired reality and the path between them is not immediately obvious. Some problems are simple: a broken appliance needs repair or replacement. Others are complex: you need to choose between career paths with different tradeoffs, or you must address a deteriorating relationship. Complex problems often lack single correct solutions and involve multiple stakeholders, competing priorities, or incomplete information.

Distinguish between problems you can solve and circumstances you must accept. Some situations are genuinely beyond your control. You cannot change other people's behavior through force of will, reverse past decisions, or prevent all negative events. Attempting to solve unsolvable problems creates frustration and wastes resources. Focus your problem-solving efforts on situations where your actions can meaningfully affect outcomes.

Many clear problems are symptoms of underlying issues. Chronic lateness might reflect poor time estimation, disorganization, or subconscious ambivalence about commitments. Repeated conflicts with coworkers might stem from unclear communication norms or incompatible work styles. Addressing symptoms provides only temporary relief; finding and addressing root causes produces lasting improvement.

Step One: Define the Problem Clearly

Effective problem-solving begins with clear problem definition. Vague problem statements like "everything is overwhelming" or "my life is not working" are too broad to address productively. Specific definition focuses your efforts and makes solutions identifiable.

Ask yourself what specifically is wrong. What observable facts show that a problem exists? What is the current situation? What would you prefer instead? Be precise. "I need a better job" is vague. "I need to increase my income by $10,000 annually to cover living expenses without accumulating debt" or "I need work that allows flexible hours because my current schedule conflicts with family responsibilities" shows concrete problems you can address.

Describe problems in neutral, factual terms rather than emotionally charged language. "My roommate is a selfish jerk" does not clarify the actual problem. "My roommate consistently plays loud music after 11pm despite our agreement to maintain quiet hours" shows a specific issue you can address. Emotional language escalates conflict and obscures the actual problem.

Verify that you are addressing the actual problem rather than reacting to surface symptoms. If you are constantly exhausted, the problem might not be lack of sleep but rather poor stress management, health issues, or taking on too many commitments. If you struggle to save money, the problem might not be insufficient income but rather unclear financial priorities or impulsive spending patterns. Taking time to understand root causes prevents you from implementing solutions that address symptoms while leaving underlying problems unresolved.

Step Two: Gather Relevant Information

Most problems cannot be solved effectively without adequate information. Find what information would help you understand the problem better or evaluate potential solutions, then systematically gather it.

Decide what you know, what you do not know, and what you need to know. Make these distinctions explicit. You may know that your car is making an unusual noise and that continuing to drive could cause damage. You may not know what is causing the noise or how urgent repair is. You need to know what the problem is and what repair will cost so you can decide whether to fix it at once or save money first.

Seek information from reliable sources. For technical problems, consult people with relevant ability or authoritative references. For interpersonal problems, consider multiple perspectives rather than assuming your first interpretation is complete. For decisions about unfamiliar situations, research what others who have faced similar circumstances learned.

Be aware of cognitive biases that affect information gathering. Confirmation bias leads you to preferentially seek information supporting your existing beliefs while dismissing contradictory evidence. Availability bias causes you to overweight information that is easily recalled, which may not be representative. Actively look for information that challenges your assumptions.

Consider alternative explanations for observations. Ask people with different perspectives for their views.

Recognize when you have sufficient information to continue. Perfect information is rarely available. Gathering information indefinitely delays action and itself has costs. At some point, you have enough information to make a reasonable decision even if uncertainty stays. Balance thoroughness against timeliness.

Step Three: Identify What You Can Control

Distinguish clearly between factors you can influence and factors you cannot. Focusing energy on things outside your control generates frustration without producing results. Directing attention to controllable factors increases effectiveness.

You control your own actions, decisions, and responses. You can change your behavior, develop new skills, alter how you spend time and money, and choose how you respond to external circumstances. You have significant influence over these domains.

You cannot control other people's feelings, thoughts, or choices. You may be able to influence them through requests, incentives, or clear communication about consequences, but ultimately, they decide their own behavior. You cannot control past events, broad economic conditions, weather, organizational policies set by others, or random chance.

Many situations involve partial control. You cannot control whether you are hired for a specific job, but you can control the quality of your application and interview preparation. You cannot control whether a relationship partner chooses to change problematic behavior, but you can control whether you are still in that relationship and what boundaries you set up. Finding where your control exists within partially controllable situations helps you focus effort productively.

Reframe problems in terms of your available options. Instead of "How do I make my boss stop micromanaging me?" ask "Given that my boss micromanages, what can I do to minimize its impact on my work satisfaction?" The first question focuses on changing something outside your control. The second focuses on your response, which is within your control. This shift often reveals actionable solutions where none seemed to exist.

Step Four: Generate Multiple Potential Solutions

Resist the temptation to implement the first solution that occurs to you. Better solutions often appear from considering multiple approaches before deciding. The quality of your solution set limits the quality of your ultimate choice.

Brainstorm without immediately evaluating feasibility. In this phase, generate ideas without censoring them. Impractical ideas sometimes have elements that can be adapted into workable solutions. Premature evaluation shuts down creative thinking.

Consider solutions from different categories. If facing a money problem, solutions might involve increasing income, decreasing expenses, negotiating payment terms, or restructuring debt. Each category of solution has different implementation requirements and trade-offs. Limiting yourself to one category constrains your options unnecessarily.

Think through what has worked in similar situations for you or others. Past experience is valuable. However, avoid assuming that what worked before will work now if circumstances have changed significantly.

Ask other people for suggestions. They may have insights or experience you lack. Explaining the problem to someone else often clarifies your own thinking even if they do not suggest novel solutions.

Include a "do nothing" option in your solution set. Sometimes the costs of acting outweigh the benefits. Explicitly considering inaction as a possibility helps you evaluate whether a problem actually requires solution or whether accepting current circumstances makes more sense.

Step Five: Evaluate Options Objectively

After generating potential solutions, evaluate each systematically against clear criteria. This prevents you from selecting options based on first appeal without considering likely outcomes.

Find criteria that matter for this specific problem. Criteria might include cost, time needed, likelihood of success, potential negative consequences, reversibility, needed resources, and impact on other priorities. Rank these criteria by importance so you know which factors should weigh most heavily in your decision.

Estimate consequences as accurately as possible. For each choice, what are likely outcomes if things go well?

What are likely outcomes if things go poorly? What is the probability of each scenario? Be honest rather than optimistic or pessimistic. Unrealistic expectations lead to poor choices.

Consider second-order effects. Your actions produce immediate consequences and also change circumstances in ways that create further consequences. If you quit a job you hate, the immediate effect is relief from daily stress. Second-order effects might include reduced income, need to find new employment, impact on career trajectory, or effects on relationships. Thinking beyond immediate outcomes improves decision quality.

Use decision matrices for complex choices. List options down the left side and criteria across the top. Rate each option on each criterion. This structured approach makes trade-offs explicit and reduces the chance that you will overlook important factors.

Check your emotional reactions to options. Strong emotional responses hold information. If a choice that seems logically best produces intense anxiety, examine why. You might be overlooking risks or values conflicts. Conversely, if a choice that seems foolish appeals strongly, explore what need it addresses that more sensible options do not. Emotions are data, not directions, but they should not be ignored.

Step Six: Implement Your Chosen Solution

After selecting an approach, implement it systematically. Many good plans fail due to poor execution. Break implementation into concrete steps. Find what needs to happen first, what resources you need, what obstacles you might meet, and how you will know whether the solution is working.

For complex solutions, create a detailed action plan. What specific actions will you take? When will you take them? What does success look like at each stage? Having clear next steps prevents implementation from stalling.

Anticipate obstacles and plan how to address them. If you are implementing a budget to reduce spending, what situations might lead you to overspend? How will you manage them? If you are asking for a raise, what objections might your manager raise? How will you respond? Preparation prevents obstacles from derailing your efforts.

Start implementation quickly while motivation is high. Delay allows enthusiasm to fade and gives you time to talk yourself out of necessary changes. Unless your solution requires extensive preparation, begin within 24 to 48 hours of deciding.

Commit to your chosen solution for a reasonable trial period before evaluating results. Many solutions require time to show effects. Changing approaches every few days prevents any approach from working. Establish how long you will persist before deciding whether your solution is effective.

Step Seven: Monitor Results and Adjust

Problem-solving does not end with implementation. Monitor whether your solution is producing desired results. If it is not, decide why and adjust accordingly.

Establish clear success metrics before implementing solutions. How will you know whether the solution is working? Be specific. If addressing chronic lateness, success means arriving on time at least 90% of days. If you improve sleep, success means sleeping seven to eight hours on weeknights. If we repair a relationship, success might mean having positive interactions more often than conflicts. Concrete metrics make evaluation possible.

Gather data objectively. Your belief of whether things are improving may be inaccurate due to selective attention or wishful thinking. Keep records where possible. Track arrival times, sleep hours, spending, or conflict frequency depending on what you are addressing. Data reveals patterns your impressions might miss.

If your solution is not working as expected, diagnose why before abandoning it. Is the approach fundamentally flawed, or is implementation inadequate? Are external circumstances preventing success, or is the problem definition incorrect? Different failure modes require different responses. Flawed approaches should be replaced. Implementation problems require better execution of the same approach. Changed circumstances may require problem redefinition.

Be willing to adapt your approach based on results. Few solutions work perfectly as initially implemented. Adjust based on what you learn. This might mean changing specific tactics while keeping overall strategy, or it might mean recognizing that your first analysis was incomplete and returning to earlier problem-solving steps.

Recognize partial success. Solutions rarely resolve problems completely on first attempt. If your solution has improved the situation even if not solving it entirely, this is progress. You can then address remaining aspects of the problem or decide whether remaining issues call for further effort.

Common Problem-Solving Errors

Understanding frequent problem-solving mistakes helps you avoid them. Several patterns appear repeatedly.

Acting impulsively without analyzing the problem wastes effort and often makes situations worse. When frustrated or anxious, the urge to do something immediately is strong. Resist this. Spend time defining the problem and gathering information before acting. An hour spent clarifying what you are actually trying to conduct prevents days spent implementing solutions to the wrong problem.

Solving symptoms rather than underlying problems produces temporary relief but does not prevent recurrence. If you repeatedly face the same type of problem, stop addressing each instance individually and find the root cause. Treating symptoms is sometimes necessary for immediate relief, but lasting solutions require addressing causes.

Allowing emotions to override analysis leads to poor decisions. Strong emotions narrow thinking and increase impulsivity. When you are angry, afraid, or anxious, delay important decisions if possible. If immediate action is necessary, consciously compensate for emotional influence by deliberately considering alternatives and consequences before acting.

Overcomplicating simple problems wastes time and energy. Not every problem requires extensive analysis. If the problem is straightforward, the solution is obvious, and the stakes are low, do not overthink it. Save sophisticated problem-solving for complex situations where it adds value.

Not following through on implemented solutions is extremely common. Initial motivation fades. Old habits reassert. External resistance appears. These obstacles are predictable. Build accountability structures, predict challenges, and keep focus on the reasons you decided to change. Successful problem-solving requires sustained effort, not just good first planning.

Attempting to solve problems outside your control creates frustration without progress. Repeatedly trying to change things you cannot control shows that you need to accept current reality and focus on what you can influence. This is not defeatism; it is efficiency.

Building Problem-Solving Capability

Problem-solving ability improves with practice. Each problem you address systematically builds your confidence and competence. Over time, structured problem-solving becomes automatic.

Start with small problems to develop the habit of systematic analysis. Do not wait for major crises to practice critical thinking skills. Addressing minor annoyances using structured approaches builds capability you can deploy when facing significant challenges.

Reflect on problem-solving experiences. After resolving a problem, consider what worked well and what you would do differently. This reflection converts experience into learning. Keep track of successful strategies so you can apply them to future problems.

Learn from others' problem-solving approaches. When colleagues, friends, or family members manage challenges effectively, see their process. What information did they gather? How did they evaluate options? What made their solution work? Studying others' successes expands your problem-solving repertoire.

Accept that some problems have no good solutions, only least-bad options. You cannot always make everything work out optimally. Sometimes you must choose between unappealing alternatives or accept tradeoffs. This is normal. The goal is not perfect outcomes but rather making the best decisions possible given available options and information.

The Road Ahead

Systematic problem-solving ability is fundamental to navigating life effectively. It allows you to address challenges proactively rather than reactively, improves decision quality, reduces stress, and builds confidence in your capacity to manage difficulties.

The problem-solving process—defining problems clearly, gathering information, finding controllable factors, generating multiple solutions, evaluating options objectively, implementing chosen approaches, and monitoring results—provides a reliable framework for addressing challenges regardless of specific content. This structure prevents common errors and increases the likelihood of effective solutions.

Problem-solving is a skill, not an innate trait. It improves with practice and conscious attention. Each problem you address systematically builds your capability to manage future challenges more effectively. Invest effort in developing this skill deliberately. The returns are large and lifelong.

Chapter 7: Strengthen Self-Awareness and Reflection

Self-awareness is understanding of your own thoughts, emotions, motivations, and behavioral patterns. It involves recognizing how you typically respond to situations, what triggers strong emotional reactions, what values guide your decisions, and how others perceive you. This understanding is foundational to effective functioning because it enables you to make deliberate choices rather than running on autopilot.

Research shows that self-awareness correlates with improved emotional regulation, better decision-making, stronger relationships, and greater life satisfaction. People with high self-awareness recognize their emotional states and understand what causes them, which allows more effective management of reactions. They understand their strengths and limitations, enabling them to use advantages while compensating for weaknesses. They align actions with values more consistently because they know what those values are.

Self-awareness is not innate. It develops through deliberate practice. This chapter addresses methods for developing self-awareness systematically and using that knowledge to improve your life.

The Components of Self-Awareness

Self-awareness encompasses several distinct dimensions. Internal self-awareness involves understanding your values, passions, behavioral patterns, reactions, and impact. External self-awareness means understanding how others perceive you. Both dimensions matter.

Emotional self-awareness means recognizing and naming your emotions accurately. Many people experience emotions without finding them precisely. They know they feel bad but cannot distinguish whether they are anxious, angry, disappointed, or something else. Accurate emotional identification is necessary for effective emotion management because different emotions call for different responses.

Values awareness means knowing what principles guide your decisions and what outcomes you care about achieving. Without clear values awareness, you may pursue goals that do not actually matter to you or make choices that contradict your stated priorities. Values clarity enables consistent decision-making and reduces regret.

Strength and weakness awareness involves honest assessment of your capabilities. Understanding what you do well allows you to seek roles and opportunities that use your strengths. Recognizing limitations helps you compensate through skill development, collaboration with others who have complementary abilities, or avoiding situations where your weaknesses will cause significant problems.

Pattern recognition means noticing recurring themes in your behavior and circumstances. You might recognize that you consistently procrastinate when facing ambiguous tasks, or that certain types of people always seem to trigger defensive reactions, or that you make poor decisions when sleep deprived. Pattern recognition allows you to predict your likely responses and intervene proactively.

Impact awareness means understanding how your actions affect others. Many conflicts stem from genuine lack of awareness about how behavior is perceived. What seems like helpful aid to you may feel like intrusive micromanagement to someone else. What feels like honest directness to you may come across as harsh criticism to others. Understanding this belief gap is crucial for effective relationships.

Regular Reflection as Foundation

Self-awareness develops through regular reflection on your experiences. Reflection means deliberately reviewing events, examining your responses, considering alternative perspectives, and extracting lessons. Without reflection, you accumulate experiences without learning from them.

Effective reflection requires structured time. Schedule regular reflection periods rather than hoping reflection will happen spontaneously. This might be 15 minutes daily, an hour weekly, or whatever frequency makes sense for your circumstances. Consistency matters more than duration.

During reflection sessions, review recent experiences systematically. What situations did you meet? How did you respond? What emotions did you experience? What worked well? What would you manage differently? Were your reactions consistent with your values and goals?

Focus on patterns rather than isolated incidents. A single instance of losing your temper is just a bad moment. Noticing that you consistently lose your temper in specific types of situations reveals a pattern you can address. Look for themes across multiple experiences.

Ask yourself specific questions to guide reflection. What challenged me this week? What am I proud of? What frustrated me, and why? When did I feel most energized? When did I feel drained? What feedback did I receive, and was it valid? What would I do differently if I could repeat this week? These questions direct attention to important aspects of experience.

Be honest during reflection. Self-deception defeats the purpose. You cannot improve based on inaccurate self-assessment. This requires intellectual humility: willingness to acknowledge mistakes, recognize limitations, and accept feedback even when uncomfortable.

Balance self-criticism with self-compassion. The goal is learning, not self-flagellation. Approach reflection with curiosity rather than judgment. When you notice problematic patterns, investigate why they occur rather than simply condemning yourself. Understanding causes enables change more effectively than harsh self-criticism.

Journaling for Self-Discovery

Written journaling is one of the most effective self-awareness tools. Writing forces you to articulate thoughts precisely, which clarifies fuzzy thinking. The act of writing engages different cognitive processes than merely thinking about experiences, often revealing insights that stay hidden during undirected thought.

Journal entries need not be lengthy or eloquent. The purpose is clarity, not literary achievement. Write whatever helps you process experiences and understand yourself better. This might be structured entries responding to specific prompts, stream-of-consciousness recording of whatever comes to mind, or brief notes about significant moments.

Write honestly. Your journal is private. No one else will read it unless you choose to share specific entries. This privacy enables the brutal honesty necessary for genuine self-examination. If you censor yourself or write as though someone else might read it, you undermine the journal's utility.

Review past entries periodically. Reading entries from weeks or months ago reveals patterns you cannot see while immersed in current circumstances. You may notice that you consistently face similar challenges, that your concerns from six months ago now seem trivial, or that you have made substantial progress on issues that felt overwhelming at the time. This long-term perspective builds confidence and finds persistent patterns worth addressing.

Some people find structured journaling prompts helpful. These might include: What am I grateful for today? What challenged me? What did I learn? What am I worried about? What went well? What would I do differently? What surprised me? These questions provide starting points when you are unsure what to write about.

Others prefer unstructured writing where they simply record whatever thoughts and feelings arise. Both approaches work. Experiment to find what feels natural and productive for you.

For specific issues, focused journaling can provide clarity. If you are struggling with a decision, write about each possibility: its advantages, disadvantages, alignment with your values, and likely consequences. If you are having recurring conflicts with someone, write about the pattern: what triggers conflicts, how you typically respond, what you might be contributing to the dynamic. Focused writing on specific topics often reveals insights that are still elusive during abstract contemplation.

Seeking and Processing Feedback

External perspective is crucial for complete self-awareness. You cannot see yourself as others see you without asking them. While self-reflection reveals your internal experience and intentions, only feedback from others reveals how you are actually perceived and what impact your behavior has.

Seek feedback actively from people whose opinions you respect and who see you in different contexts. This might include supervisors, colleagues, friends, family members, or mentors. Different people see different aspects of you, so diverse feedback sources provide more complete picture than any single perspective.

Ask specific questions rather than general requests for feedback. "Do you have any feedback for me?" is vague and often produces equally vague responses. Instead ask: "What do you think I could improve about how I communicate in meetings?" or "When we work together, what frustrates you?" or "What do you see as my biggest strength in this role?" Specific questions produce actionable feedback.

Listen to feedback without defending yourself. Your natural impulse when hearing criticism is to explain, justify, or argue. Resist this. Your job when receiving feedback is to understand the other person's perspective, not to convince them they are wrong. Even if you disagree with feedback, it still reveals how you are perceived, which is valuable information.

Ask clarifying questions to ensure you understand feedback accurately. What specific behaviors create the belief someone has described? Can they provide examples? What would improvement look like to them? Concrete details make feedback useful.

Thank people for feedback regardless of whether you agree with it. Providing honest feedback is uncomfortable. People do it because they care about your development. Expressing gratitude for their willingness to be honest encourages future feedback.

Process feedback before responding to it. If feedback triggers strong emotional reactions, take time to manage those emotions before deciding what to do with the feedback. Immediate defensive reactions often prevent you from considering whether feedback has validity.

Evaluate feedback critically. Not all feedback is correct or relevant. Consider the source: Does this person see you regularly in the relevant context? Do they have ability in the area they are commenting on? Do they have reason to be biased? Consider whether multiple people have given similar feedback, which suggests it reflects reality rather than one person's idiosyncratic feeling.

Implement feedback that seems valid. Seeking feedback is pointless if you never change based on what you learn. Find specific actions you can take to address legitimate concerns people have raised. Monitor whether these changes improve outcomes and others' beliefs.

Formal Assessment Tools

Various structured assessments can offer self-awareness insights. Personality assessments like the Big Five inventory describe your tendencies along dimensions like conscientiousness, extraversion, and emotional stability. Strengths assessments like CliftonStrengths or VIA Character Strengths find your natural capabilities. Values assessments help clarify what matters most to you.

These assessments have limitations. They provide frameworks for thinking about yourself but do not reveal absolute truth. Treat results as hypotheses to evaluate rather than definitive answers. Do assessment results match your experience? Do they help you understand patterns in your life? Do they provide useful language for discussing aspects of yourself with others?

Assessment results are most valuable when discussed with others. Comparing how you see yourself to how others see you reveals belief gaps. Having shared language from assessments eases these conversations. For example, learning that you score high on conscientiousness while your colleague scores high on flexibility helps both of you understand why you approach projects differently.

Use assessment results to find development opportunities. If an assessment reveals that you score low on a trait that matters for your goals, this suggests an area worth working on. If results confirm strengths you suspected, this confirms pursuing opportunities that use those strengths.

Understanding Your Triggers and Patterns

Triggers are situations, stimuli, or interactions that consistently provoke strong emotional or behavioral responses. Understanding your triggers allows you to predict reactions and manage them more effectively.

Common triggers include feeling dismissed or ignored, perceived unfairness, criticism of your competence, uncertainty about expectations, time pressure, and conflict. Your specific triggers relate to your values, past experiences, and sensitivities.

Find triggers by tracking when you experience intense emotions. When you feel suddenly angry, defensive, anxious, or shut down, pause to find what preceded that reaction. What was said? What happened? What did you perceive? Over time, you will notice patterns in what situations provoke strong responses.

Understanding why something triggers you helps you respond more effectively. If criticism triggers defensiveness because you interpret it as evidence of incompetence, recognizing this allows you to separate criticism of specific actions from judgments about your overall ability. If uncertainty triggers anxiety because you fear making mistakes, recognizing this allows you to develop tolerance for ambiguity rather than avoiding uncertain situations entirely.

Once you find triggers, you can prepare strategies for managing them. This might mean taking a pause before responding when triggered, reframing situations cognitively, seeking clarification when you feel uncertain, or setting up boundaries around particularly difficult triggers.

Behavioral patterns are recurring sequences in how you respond to situations. Common problematic patterns include procrastination when facing ambiguous tasks, conflict avoidance that allows problems to escalate, people-pleasing that leads to overcommitment, or perfectionism that prevents completion.

Recognizing patterns requires stepping back from individual instances to see themes. Journaling and reflection help this. When you notice yourself procrastinating again, ask what the task has in common with other tasks you procrastinate on. When you find yourself in another draining relationship, ask what this relationship has in common with earlier similar relationships. Pattern recognition reveals what aspects of situations trigger particular responses.

Many patterns developed for good reasons initially but outlived their usefulness. Perhaps you learned to avoid conflict because expressing disagreement led to punishment as a child. This was adaptive then but may be maladaptive now in adult relationships where direct communication is expected. Understanding where patterns originated helps you decide whether they still serve you.

Clarifying Your Values

Values are principles that guide decisions and define what matters to you. People often believe they know their values but have not examined them explicitly. Making values conscious and prioritizing them clarifies decision-making.

Common values include achievement, autonomy, creativity, fairness, financial security, health, helping others, learning, relationships, status, and many others.

Most people value multiple things, which creates no problems until values conflict, and you must choose which takes priority.

Clarify values by examining past decisions and their outcomes. When have you felt most satisfied with choices you made? What values were you honoring? When have you felt regret or dissatisfaction? What values did you compromise? These questions reveal what actually matters to you beyond what you think should matter.

Notice where you invest time, energy, and money. These investments reveal your actual priorities, which may differ from your stated priorities. If you claim relationships are your highest value but consistently choose to work over time with family and friends, your actual priorities may be achievement or financial security. This is not wrong, but clarity about actual values helps you make choices deliberately.

Rank your values explicitly. When two values conflict, which takes precedence? You cannot maximize all values simultaneously. Clear prioritization simplifies difficult decisions. If autonomy ranks higher than security for you, you may choose a risky opportunity over a stable situation. If security ranks higher, you make the opposite choice. Neither is wrong but knowing your priorities cuts indecision.

Revisit values periodically. They may shift as your life circumstances change. Values that mattered in your early twenties may be less important a decade later. Regular reassessment ensures your choices align with current rather than outdated values.

Recognizing Cognitive Biases

Cognitive biases are systematic errors in thinking that affect everyone. Recognizing common biases in your own thinking improves decision quality.

Confirmation bias leads you to notice evidence supporting existing beliefs while dismissing contradictory evidence. When you have decided something is true, you unconsciously filter information to support that conclusion. Combat this by actively seeking information that challenges your views and taking contradictory evidence seriously.

Fundamental attribution error causes you to explain others' behavior as reflecting their character while explaining your own behavior as responding to circumstances. When someone else is late, you conclude they are disorganized. When you are late, you know it was due to unexpected traffic. Recognizing this asymmetry increases empathy and reduces interpersonal conflict.

Sunk cost fallacy causes you to continue investing in failing endeavors because you have already invested significantly. The past investment is gone regardless of what you do now, but psychologically it feels wasteful to abandon something you have spent time, money, or effort on. Recognize that the relevant question is whether future investment will produce valuable returns, not whether past investment was large.

Availability bias causes you to overweight information that is easily recalled, which is typically recent, vivid, or emotionally significant information. This leads to inaccurate probability estimates. After hearing about a plane crash, you may overestimate air travel risk despite planes being statistically safe. Deliberately seek statistical information rather than relying on anecdotes.

Dunning-Kruger effect describes how people with limited knowledge in an area overestimate their competence while experts underestimate theirs. When you know little about something, you lack knowledge of what you do not know, creating false confidence. Recognizing this helps you seek ability appropriately and acknowledge limitations.

Being aware of biases does not end them. They are features of human cognition, not personal failings. However, awareness allows you to compensate. When making important decisions, deliberately check whether biases might be influencing your thinking. Seek outside perspectives. Gather data that might contradict your intuition. These practices reduce bias effects even though biases themselves persist.

Emotional Awareness and Regulation

Emotional awareness means recognizing and accurately labeling your emotional states. Many people experience emotions without finding them precisely, which impairs their ability to respond effectively.

Develop richer emotional vocabulary. Expand beyond broad categories like happy, sad, and angry. Learn to distinguish anxiety from fear, disappointment from sadness, frustration from anger, satisfaction from pride, curiosity from confusion. More precise emotional identification enables more targeted responses.

Notice physical sensations associated with emotions. Different emotions produce different bodily states.

Anxiety might manifest as tightness in your chest, tension in your shoulders, or churning in your stomach. Anger might produce clenched jaw, heat in your face, or energized feeling. Recognizing these physical signals allows earlier emotion detection, which makes regulation easier.

Understand that emotions hold information about how you are interpreting situations. Fear shows that you perceive threat. Anger shows that you perceive unfairness or boundary violation. Guilt shows that you have acted inconsistently with your values. Disappointment shows that reality has fallen short of expectations. Decoding what emotions signal helps you address underlying concerns rather than just managing symptoms.

Emotional regulation does not mean suppression. Healthy regulation involves experiencing emotions fully while managing behavioral responses. You can feel angry without yelling at someone. You can feel anxious without avoiding challenges. You can feel sad without becoming nonfunctional. The goal is experiencing emotions without being controlled by them.

Strategies for emotional regulation include: pausing before responding to allow initial intensity to decrease; reappraising situations to change emotional responses; using physical activity to discharge emotional arousal; talking through feelings with trusted others; and engaging in activities that shift mood states. Different strategies work for different people and different emotions. Experiment to find what works for you.

Accept that some emotional discomfort is inevitable and healthy. You cannot and should not try to keep constant positive emotion. Negative emotions serve adaptive functions. Anxiety motivates preparation. Guilt motivates repairing harm you have caused. Sadness signals loss and elicits support from others. The goal is not ending negative emotions but responding to them constructively.

Understanding How Others Perceive You

How others perceive you affects your opportunities and relationships. Your intentions matter, but so does your impact. Someone may not intend to be intimidating, but if others consistently feel intimidated, this creates real problems regardless of intent.

Belief gaps are common. You experience your internal state: your intentions, your constraints, your reasoning. Others experience only your observable behavior and must infer what drives it. They may reach different conclusions than what you intended to convey.

You might think you are being helpful; others might perceive you as controlling. You might think you are being thorough; others might perceive you as indecisive. You might think you are being efficient with words; others might perceive you as curt. These gaps cause interpersonal problems.

Reduce belief gaps by asking how you come across to others. When someone seems to react negatively to you, ask what created that reaction. When you receive feedback about how you are perceived, take it seriously even if it differs from your self-perception. Other people's beliefs are their reality, and you must work with that reality regardless of whether you think it is correct.

Pay attention to patterns in how different people describe you. If one person says you are interrupting, perhaps that person is overly sensitive. If multiple people independently say you interrupt, you probably interrupt more than you realize. Recurring themes in feedback signal real patterns worth addressing.

Video record yourself in relevant situations when possible. Watching yourself in meetings, presentations, or conversations often reveals mannerisms, speech patterns, or behaviors you were unaware of. Seeing yourself as others see you provides perspective that is otherwise difficult to obtain.

Using Self-Knowledge for Better Decisions

Self-awareness value is in applying it. Understanding yourself helps you make better choices about career, relationships, how you spend time, and how you respond to challenges.

Choose environments that fit your working style. If you know you need quiet to concentrate, seek workspaces where that is available. If you know you need social interaction to support energy, avoid highly isolated roles. If you know you perform best with structure, seek situations providing clear expectations. Fitting environment to your needs produces better outcomes than trying to force yourself to thrive in incompatible environments.

Select goals aligned with your values. When you pursue goals inconsistent with what matters to you, achievement feels hollow. When goals align with values, effort feels meaningful even when difficult. Knowing your values prevents you from pursuing accomplishments that do not actually satisfy you.

Leverage your strengths while managing your weaknesses. Focus effort on developing areas where you have natural aptitude rather than trying to become average at everything. When possible, delegate or collaborate with others in areas where you are weak. This is more efficient than endless struggle against your natural inclinations.

Anticipate situations that trigger problematic responses and prepare accordingly. If you know you become defensive when criticized, prepare to pause and listen before responding. If you know you make poor decisions when tired, avoid scheduling important decisions during times when you are typically fatigued. If you know you overspend when stressed, remove temptations during high-stress periods. Knowing your vulnerabilities allows proactive management.

Choose relationships deliberately. Understanding what types of people and relationship dynamics work well for you helps you invest in relationships likely to be mutually beneficial while avoiding patterns that consistently cause problems. If you know you need direct communication, seek people who communicate that way. If you know you struggle with highly emotional people, recognize that and set proper boundaries.

Ongoing Development

Self-awareness is not a destination but an ongoing practice. You continue learning about yourself throughout your life as you meet new situations and as you yourself change over time.

Maintain regular reflection practice. Schedule time for it. Protect that time from competing demands. Treat self-awareness development as seriously as any other important commitment.

Remain curious about yourself. When you notice unexpected reactions, explore why they occurred rather than dismissing them. When you receive surprising feedback, investigate what led to that feeling rather than rejecting it. Curiosity fuels continuous self-discovery.

Accept that self-awareness sometimes reveals uncomfortable truths. You might discover you value things you wish did not matter to you. You might recognize patterns you wish you did not have. You might face evidence that your self-concept needs revision. This discomfort is part of growth. Accurate self-knowledge, even when uncomfortable, is more useful than flattering self-deception.

Share your self-awareness journey with trusted others. Discussing what you are learning about yourself deepens understanding and creates accountability. Others can help you see blind spots and test whether your self-assessments match their observations.

The Road Ahead

Self-awareness is foundational to effective living. Understanding your thoughts, emotions, values, patterns, triggers, strengths, and limitations enables deliberate choices rather than reactive responses. This understanding improves emotional regulation, decision quality, relationship success, and overall life satisfaction.

Developing self-awareness requires deliberate practice through regular reflection, journaling, seeking feedback, using assessment tools, and studying your patterns over time. The investment is substantial, but the returns are proportionally large. Almost every aspect of your life improves when you understand yourself more accurately.

Self-awareness is not self-absorption. The goal is not endless navel-gazing but rather developing understanding that enables more effective action. You reflect in order to learn. You learn in order to improve. You improve in order to achieve your goals and live according to your values. Self-awareness is the tool; a life well-lived is the outcome.

Chapter 8: Foster Flexibility and Open-Mindedness

Flexibility and open-mindedness are the capacity to adapt your thinking and behavior when circumstances change or when confronted with new information. These qualities enable you to function effectively in uncertain environments, support productive relationships with people whose perspectives differ from yours, and continue learning throughout your life.

Many people confuse flexibility with lack of conviction or standards. This is incorrect. Flexibility means adapting means while keeping important ends. It means being willing to revise beliefs when evidence contradicts them. It means considering alternatives before committing to approaches. It does not mean abandoning values or accepting anything without evaluation.

Research in organizational behavior, psychology, and education consistently shows that cognitive flexibility predicts success across domains. Flexible thinkers solve novel problems more effectively, adapt to changing circumstances more readily, and support better relationships because they can understand perspectives different from their own.

Understanding Cognitive Flexibility

Cognitive flexibility is the mental capacity to switch between thinking about different concepts or to think about multiple concepts simultaneously. It allows you to consider problems from multiple angles, adapt strategies when initial approaches fail, and integrate seemingly contradictory information into coherent understanding.

Flexible thinking contrasts with rigid thinking, where you apply the same approach regardless of whether it fits the situation, hold beliefs regardless of contradictory evidence, or refuse to consider alternatives. Rigid thinking develops when you meet situations repeatedly that call for the same response. The pattern becomes automatic, which is efficient for familiar situations but problematic for novel ones requiring different approaches.

Cognitive flexibility exists on a continuum. Everyone shows more flexibility in some domains than others. You might be highly flexible about method but rigid about core values. You might readily adopt new technologies but resist changing social habits. Understanding where you tend toward rigidity helps you compensate in those areas.

Benefits of Flexible Thinking

Flexible thinkers excel at problem-solving because they can generate multiple potential solutions rather than fixating on a single approach. When one strategy fails, they can quickly pivot to alternatives. This adaptability is particularly valuable when dealing with complex problems that have no obvious solutions or when running in rapidly changing environments.

Flexibility improves decision-making. Rigid thinkers often make decisions based on limited information because they cannot tolerate ambiguity. Flexible thinkers can sit with uncertainty while gathering more information, consider multiple perspectives before deciding, and revise decisions when circumstances change. This produces better long-term outcomes even though it may feel slower initially.

Relationships receive help from flexibility. People differ in values, communication styles, preferences, and needs. Rigid expectations about how others should behave create constant conflict. Flexible approaches to relationships mean adapting your communication style to what works for different people, negotiating compromises, and accepting that people can meet your needs in different ways than you initially expected.

Learning requires flexibility. New information often contradicts existing beliefs. Flexible learners can revise their understanding when presented with contradictory evidence. Rigid learners either reject new information that does not fit existing frameworks or compartmentalize it without integrating it into their broader understanding. This limits their capacity to develop ability.

Career success increasingly depends on adaptability. Technology changes, industries evolve, organizational structures shift, and job requirements transform. Workers who can learn new skills, adapt to different roles, and change their approaches to fit new contexts keep employment security. Those who insist on doing things as they always have face obsolescence.

Recognizing Rigid Thinking Patterns

Finding your own rigid thinking patterns is the first step toward developing flexibility. Common indicators include repeatedly meeting the same problems despite trying to solve them, difficulty collaborating with people who have different styles, resistance to new approaches, and inability to see multiple sides of issues.

All-or-nothing thinking is a rigid pattern where you categorize situations, people, or outcomes as entirely good or entirely bad with no middle ground. This prevents nuanced understanding. Most situations are mixed: they have both advantages and disadvantages, both risks and opportunities. Inability to recognize this complexity leads to poor decisions.

Overgeneralization means drawing broad conclusions from limited evidence. One bad experience with a particular approach leads you to conclude the approach never works. One difficult interaction with someone who shares certain characteristics leads you to avoid everyone with those characteristics. This rigidity prevents you from recognizing when circumstances differ from past experiences.

Rules-based thinking applied inflexibly causes problems. Rules are useful heuristics for common situations, but most rules have exceptions. Insisting that rules apply universally regardless of context shows rigidity. Flexible thinkers understand principles underlying rules and can judge when exceptions are proper.

Defensive responses to feedback show rigidity. If you immediately justify your behavior, explain why criticism is wrong, or dismiss feedback without considering its validity, you are showing inflexible thinking. Flexible thinkers can hear feedback, consider whether it is correct, and adjust behavior accordingly even when initial reaction is defensive.

Notice situations where you feel stuck or frustrated by unchanging circumstances. Often these situations persist because you are repeatedly applying the same ineffective approach. The definition of insanity is trying the same action while expecting different results. If you find yourself in this pattern, you need more flexible thinking.

Developing Mental Flexibility

Flexibility develops through deliberate practice. Like physical flexibility, mental flexibility improves when you regularly stretch beyond comfortable ranges.

Actively seek perspectives different from your own. Read arguments for positions you disagree with. Talk to people who have different backgrounds, values, or political views. The goal is not necessarily changing your mind but understanding how reasonable people can reach different conclusions. This practice builds capacity to see multiple sides of issues.

When you meet ideas that contradict your beliefs, pause before rejecting them. Ask yourself: What would have to be true for this perspective to make sense? What evidence would change my mind? If you cannot articulate what evidence would alter your position, you are holding beliefs dogmatically rather than rationally. Flexible thinking requires being able to specify conditions under which you would revise your views.

Practice generating multiple solutions to problems before selecting one. When facing a challenge, brainstorm at least three different approaches before evaluating which is best. This prevents premature commitment to your first idea and builds the habit of considering alternatives.

Experiment with different approaches in low-stakes situations. If you always plan extensively before acting, try responding more spontaneously in situations where mistakes will not be costly. If you typically act impulsively, practice deliberation on minor decisions. These experiments build flexibility by forcing you outside habitual patterns.

Learn new skills, particularly ones that are significantly different from your existing capabilities. Learning develops neural plasticity generally, not just in the specific domain of study. If your work is highly analytical, learn a creative skill. If your ability is verbal, study something quantitative. These cognitive challenges build general flexibility.

Deliberately change your environment. Take different routes to familiar destinations. Rearrange your workspace. Shop at different stores. These small changes disrupt autopilot functioning and require conscious adaptation. While individually minor, they cumulatively build flexibility.

Maintaining Standards While Remaining Open

Flexibility does not mean abandoning standards or accepting everything uncritically. The concern that being open-minded means believing anything or tolerating everything causes many people to resist developing flexibility. This concern is misguided.

Distinguish between core values and instrumental preferences. Core values are fundamental principles that guide your most important decisions. These should be stable. Instrumental preferences are ways of achieving your values. These should be flexible. For example, if you value honesty, this core value stays constant. But how you express honesty appropriately might differ across contexts: what is proper directness with close friends might be inappropriate bluntness with colleagues. Adapting expression to context shows flexibility, not compromise of values.

Evidence-based belief revision is not weakness. When substantial evidence contradicts your beliefs, revising those beliefs shows intellectual integrity, not lack of conviction. Refusing to change beliefs despite contradictory evidence is not principled; it is dogmatic. Flexible thinkers update their beliefs as they gather more information.

Evaluate ideas on their merits rather than their source. People you generally disagree with can still have valid points on specific issues. People whose overall approach you admire can still be wrong about particular things. Flexible thinking means assessing individual claims independently rather than accepting or rejecting them based on whether you like the person making them.

Be willing to say "I don't know" or "I'm not sure yet." Rigid thinkers feel compelled to have firm opinions about everything. Flexible thinkers can acknowledge uncertainty. In fact, acknowledging uncertainty is often more intellectually honest than forcing premature conclusions based on insufficient information.

Develop decision-making criteria that help you distinguish when to hold firm and when to adapt. These criteria might include: Does this involve a core value or an instrumental preference? Will this decision have major or minor consequences? Is new information genuinely novel or just a different framing of what I already knew? Am I resisting change because I have good reasons or simply because change is uncomfortable? Explicit criteria prevent arbitrary flexibility or stubbornness.

Seeking Diverse Perspectives

Exposure to diverse perspectives is among the most effective ways to develop flexible thinking. When you regularly meet people who see the world differently than you do, you cannot keep the illusion that your way is the only reasonable way.

Seek diversity along multiple dimensions: different cultural backgrounds, different professional ability, different life experiences, different values and political views. Each type of diversity offers different insights. Someone from a different culture may notice assumptions you make unconsciously. Someone in a different profession may have methodologies applicable to your work. Someone who has overcome challenges you have not faced may have strategies you can adapt.

When engaging with people who have different perspectives, focus on understanding rather than debating. Ask questions about their reasoning: What experiences led them to this conclusion? What evidence do they find persuasive? What are they trying to achieve? Understanding does not require agreement. You can accurately grasp someone's perspective while still disagreeing with it. But you cannot evaluate a perspective fairly if you do not first understand it.

Notice when you dismiss others' views without genuine consideration. If you immediately categorize an idea as wrong because of who said it or because it conflicts with your existing beliefs, you are showing rigid thinking. Train yourself to at least consider ideas before rejecting them. Ask: What might someone find valuable about this perspective? Under what circumstances might this approach work? What am I missing?

Build relationships with people who think differently than you do. This provides regular exposure to alternative viewpoints and makes it harder to caricature perspectives you disagree with. It is easier to dismiss abstract political positions than to dismiss thoughtful analysis from someone you respect.

Adapting to Changing Circumstances

Circumstances change constantly. Strategies that worked in one context may fail in another. Flexibility means recognizing when adaptation is necessary and implementing it promptly.

Monitor whether your approaches are producing desired results. If outcomes are deteriorating despite consistent effort, circumstances have likely changed in ways that require different strategies. Continuing the same approach harder is rarely the solution. You need different tactics.

Distinguish between situations requiring persistence and situations requiring adaptation. Some goals take sustained effort over long periods, and giving up prematurely prevents success. Others are genuinely unachievable given current circumstances, and continuing to pursue them wastes resources. This distinction is not always clear, but patterns appear. If multiple alternative approaches all fail despite good execution, external barriers may be insurmountable. If you have not genuinely tried alternatives, your current approach may simply be wrong.

Accept that plans will need revision. No plan survives first contact with reality unchanged. When you meet obstacles, ask whether they show fundamental flaws in your plan or simply need tactical adjustments. Major strategic shifts require careful thought. Minor tactical adjustments should happen fluidly as you gather information about what works.

Develop contingency plans for predictable uncertainties. While you cannot plan for every possibility, you can prepare for common complications. What will you do if your first choice for post-graduation plans does not work out? If a project takes longer than expected? If a key resource becomes unavailable? Having thought through alternatives makes adaptation faster when needed.

View change as opportunity rather than threat. This is easier said than done, particularly when change is not your choice. But change creates opportunities for people who can adapt quickly. Skills become more valuable when they are scarce. Being among the first to master new approaches or technologies provides competitive advantage. Training yourself to look for opportunities within change reduces anxiety and improves response.

Balancing Conviction with Openness

The challenge is keeping strong convictions about important matters while staying open to revision when evidence calls for it. This is not a contradiction but a sophisticated balance.

Hold beliefs proportional to evidence. Beliefs supported by substantial evidence call for strong conviction. Beliefs based on limited evidence or personal preference should be held more tentatively. This proportionality means you have firm convictions about some things while staying uncertain about others. Both strong belief and acknowledged uncertainty can coexist.

Distinguish confidence in values from confidence in factual claims. You can be absolutely committed to values like honesty or fairness while staying open about the best ways to implement those values in specific situations. Values commitment provides direction; factual flexibility provides adaptation.

Be willing to defend your views while also being willing to revise them. These are not opposites. You can vigorously argue for your position while simultaneously being open to persuasive counterarguments. In fact, confident people are generally more open to revising beliefs because they are not threatened by the possibility of being wrong. Their self-worth is not dependent on being right about every specific question.

Intellectual humility is not the same as lack of confidence. Intellectual humility means recognizing the limits of your knowledge and being willing to learn. This is consistent with confidence in areas where you do have ability. You can be confident in your professional competence while humbly acknowledging that people in other fields know things you do not.

The Road Ahead

Flexibility and open-mindedness are essential for navigating complex, changing environments. They enable effective problem-solving, support continuous learning, ease productive relationships, and allow adaptation to new circumstances. These qualities are not weaknesses but sophisticated cognitive capabilities.

Developing flexibility requires deliberate practice: seeking diverse perspectives, considering alternatives before deciding, experimenting with different approaches, and being willing to revise beliefs when evidence calls for. This does not mean abandoning standards or accepting everything uncritically. It means keeping firm values while adapting methods, holding beliefs proportional to evidence, and balancing conviction with openness.

The alternative to flexibility is increasing obsolescence as the world changes around you. Rigid thinkers struggle with novel problems, do not learn from new information, and experience unnecessary interpersonal conflict. Flexible thinkers thrive in uncertainty, continue developing throughout their lives, and support effectiveness across diverse situations. The choice is clear.

Chapter 9: Develop Healthy Lifestyle Habits

Physical health and mental health are interconnected. Neglecting physical needs undermines psychological functioning. Poor sleep impairs decision-making and emotional regulation. Inadequate nutrition affects mood and cognitive performance. Lack of physical activity increases anxiety and depression. Conversely, supporting health through proper sleep, nutrition, exercise, and stress management builds resilience and supports best performance.

Many people treat health maintenance as optional or postponable until problems appear. This is short-sighted. Prevention is more effective and less costly than treatment. Establishing healthy habits early creates foundations for sustained wellbeing. Poor habits compound over time, making later correction increasingly difficult.

This chapter addresses fundamental health practices that directly affect your capacity to manage challenges, keep energy, regulate emotions, and perform effectively.

Sleep Requirements and Hygiene

Sleep is not optional. It is a biological necessity. During sleep, your brain combines memories, processes emotions, removes metabolic waste, and performs essential maintenance. Insufficient sleep impairs cognitive function, weakens immune response, disrupts emotional regulation, and increases risk of chronic diseases.

Adults need seven to nine hours of sleep nightly. Individual needs vary within this range, but very few people truly function optimally on less than seven hours despite commonly claiming they do. Sleep deprivation accumulates; you cannot consistently sleep six hours nightly and support full cognitive function by sleeping extra on weekends.

Quality matters as much as quantity. Interrupted sleep or sleep disrupted by substances provides less restoration than uninterrupted sleep. Deep sleep and REM sleep serve different essential functions. Fragmenting sleep across multiple periods is less restorative than combined sleep.

Sleep hygiene refers to practices that promote consistent, good-quality sleep. Maintain consistent sleep and wake times, including weekends. Your circadian rhythm functions best with regularity. Shifting sleep schedules on weekends creates jet lag effects that impair functioning early in the week.

Create an environment conducive to sleep. Your bedroom should be dark, quiet, and cool. Light suppresses melatonin production, which delays sleep onset. Noise disrupts sleep even when you do not consciously wake. Temperature affects sleep quality; most people sleep best in rooms between 60 and 67 degrees Fahrenheit.

Avoid screens for at least one hour before bed. The blue light emitted by phones, tablets, and computers suppresses melatonin production. Additionally, engaging content keeps your mind active when you should be winding down. If you must use screens near bedtime, use blue light filters and choose calming content.

Avoid caffeine for at least six hours before bed. Caffeine has a half-life of approximately five to six hours, meaning half is still in your system six hours after consumption. Consuming caffeine in the afternoon or evening interferes with sleep onset and reduces sleep quality even if you manage to fall asleep.

Avoid alcohol near bedtime. While alcohol may help you fall asleep initially, it disrupts sleep architecture, reducing REM sleep and causing lighter, more fragmented sleep later in the night. You may spend more time in bed but obtain less restorative sleep.

Exercise regularly, but not within three hours of bedtime. Physical activity improves sleep quality but exercising too close to bedtime can interfere with sleep onset due to elevated core body temperature and alertness.

If you cannot fall asleep within 20 minutes, get up and do a quiet, non-stimulating activity until you feel sleepy. Lying awake in bed conditions your brain to associate bed with wakefulness rather than sleep. Breaking this association by getting up prevents the problem from worsening.

This lifestyle habit is revisited in detail in Chapter 13: Get Enough Sleep.

Nutrition Fundamentals

Nutrition affects energy levels, cognitive function, mood, immune function, and long-term health. Your body requires specific nutrients to function optimally. While individual dietary needs vary based on genetics, activity level, and health status, certain principles apply broadly.

Eat predominantly whole, minimally processed foods. Fruits, vegetables, whole grains, legumes, nuts, seeds, lean proteins, and healthy fats should form the foundation of your diet. These foods provide essential nutrients, fiber, and beneficial compounds while generally being less calorie-dense than processed foods.

Processed foods often have excessive sodium, sugar, and unhealthy fats while being stripped of fiber and micronutrients. While occasional consumption is fine, basing your diet on processed foods leads to poor nutrition, unstable energy, and increased disease risk.

Aim for dietary diversity. Different foods provide different nutrients. Eating a variety of foods increases the likelihood of obtaining all necessary nutrients without requiring extensive nutrition knowledge or supplementation. Include different colored vegetables, various protein sources, and multiple types of whole grains.

Pay attention to hunger and fullness cues. Eat when hungry; stop when satisfied. This sounds simple but modern food environment makes it difficult. Highly palatable processed foods override natural satiety signals. Large portions and eating while distracted lead to overconsumption. Mindful eating—paying attention to what and how much you consume—helps support proper intake.

Stay adequately hydrated. Water is essential for virtually every bodily function. Thirst is not always a reliable indicator of hydration status. Aim for approximately half your body weight in ounces of water daily, more if you exercise heavily or live in hot climates. Other beverages contribute to hydration, but water should be your primary fluid source.

Plan meals and snacks in advance when possible. Having healthy food readily available prevents resorting to convenience options that are typically less nutritious. Meal preparation on weekends or evenings when you have time ensures you have good options during busy periods.

Be realistic about dietary changes. Attempting to overhaul your entire diet overnight is rarely sustainable. Make incremental improvements. Add a serving of vegetables to meals you already eat. Replace one processed snack with a whole food alternative. Gradually transition toward healthier patterns rather than expecting immediate perfection.

Avoid restrictive dieting unless medically necessary. Severe calorie restriction, elimination of entire food groups without medical reason, or rigid food rules often lead to disordered eating patterns. Focus on eating nutritious foods in proper amounts rather than on restriction and deprivation.

Physical Activity Requirements

Regular physical activity is essential for health. Exercise provides benefits beyond physical fitness: it improves mood, reduces anxiety and depression, enhances cognitive function, promotes better sleep, and builds stress resilience.

Current recommendations call for at least 150 minutes of moderate-intensity aerobic activity or 75 minutes of vigorous-intensity activity weekly, plus strength training at least twice weekly. This translates to 30 minutes of moderate activity five days per week or 25 minutes of vigorous activity three days per week, plus two strength sessions.

Moderate-intensity activity includes brisk walking, recreational swimming, doubles tennis, or active recreational activities where you can talk but not sing. Vigorous-intensity activity includes running, swimming laps, singles tennis, or other activities where conversation is difficult. Both intensity levels provide health benefits.

Strength training involves exercises that work major muscle groups: legs, hips, back, chest, shoulders, and arms. This might include weight lifting, resistance band exercises, bodyweight exercises, or activities like rock climbing. Strength training keeps muscle mass, supports bone density, improves metabolism, and reduces injury risk.

Any movement is better than none. If you currently do little physical activity, start where you are and gradually increase. Even short bouts of activity provide benefits. Take stairs instead of elevators. Walk during breaks. Do bodyweight exercises during commercial breaks. These small activities accumulate.

Choose activities you enjoy. You are more likely to keep exercise that is pleasant rather than viewing it as punishment. Experiment with different activities to find what suits you. Some people thrive in group fitness classes; others prefer solitary activities. Some enjoy competitive sports; others prefer individual challenges. Find your preference and build on it.

Make physical activity convenient. Reduce barriers to exercising. Keep workout clothes accessible. Choose gyms or activities close to home or work. Schedule exercise appointments just as you schedule other commitments. Easier access increases consistency.

Vary your activities to prevent boredom and reduce overuse injury risk. Cross-training, using different activities on different days, allows recovery for specific muscle groups while supporting overall fitness. It also keeps exercise interesting.

Stress Management Techniques

Stress is inevitable. How you manage it decides whether it enhances or impairs your performance. Acute stress can improve focus and performance. Chronic unmanaged stress damages health and undermines functioning.

Find your stress symptoms. Stress manifests differently for different people: some experience physical symptoms like tension headaches or upset stomach; others experience emotional symptoms like irritability or anxiety; still others notice behavioral changes like disrupted sleep or appetite changes. Recognizing your stress signals enables earlier intervention.

Use physical activity for stress management. Exercise reduces stress hormones while increasing endorphins. Even brief physical activity—a ten-minute walk, a few minutes of stretching—can shift your physiological state and improve mood.

Practice relaxation techniques. Progressive muscle relaxation involves systematically tensing and releasing muscle groups, which reduces physical tension and promotes relaxation. Deep breathing activates the parasympathetic nervous system, countering the stress response. Guided imagery uses mental visualization to promote calm. These techniques require practice to become effective but provide powerful stress management tools.

Maintain social connections. Talking with trusted friends or family members about stressors provides emotional support and often new perspectives on problems. Social isolation increases stress and reduces your capacity to manage it.

Engage in enjoyable activities regularly, not just when stressed. Hobbies, creative pursuits, time in nature, and leisure activities provide recovery from work demands and support wellbeing. Waiting until you are overwhelmed to engage in enjoyable activities means missing their preventative benefits.

Limit exposure to unnecessary stressors when possible. You cannot end all stress, but you can reduce exposure to stressors you control. This might mean limiting news consumption if current events cause distress, setting boundaries with people who consistently increase stress, or simplifying aspects of life that create complexity without adding value.

Seek professional help when stress becomes unmanageable. If stress is impairing your functioning significantly, causes persistent physical symptoms, leads to substance use as coping mechanism, or triggers thoughts of self-harm, professional treatment is proper. There is no virtue in struggling alone with serious stress when effective treatment exists.

Avoiding Substance Abuse

Substance use exists on a continuum from casual use to dependence. Understanding where your use falls on this continuum and recognizing early warning signs of problematic patterns protects your health and functioning.

Alcohol is widely available and socially accepted, which can obscure its risks. Moderate alcohol consumption for most adults means no more than one drink daily for women or two for men. Exceeding these amounts regularly increases health risks. Binge drinking—four or more drinks for women or five for men in approximately two hours—poses particular risks including impaired judgment, injury risk, and contribution to alcohol dependence.

Use alcohol intentionally rather than habitually. If you drink to cope with stress, manage emotions, or because you feel unable to enjoy social situations without it, this suggests problematic patterns. Alcohol should be an occasional addition to activities you would enjoy anyway, not a necessary part of enjoyment or coping mechanism.

Cannabis, even where legal, affects cognitive function, particularly in young adults whose brains are still developing. Regular use can impair memory, reduce motivation, and in some individuals trigger or worsen mental health problems. If you choose to use cannabis, do so infrequently and be honest with yourself about whether use is affecting your functioning.

Avoid using substances prescribed to others. Prescription medications, particularly stimulants and opioids, carry significant risks. Using them without medical supervision is dangerous and often illegal.

Recognize early warning signs of substance problems: using more than intended, unsuccessful attempts to cut back, spending significant time obtaining or recovering from substance use, continued use despite negative consequences, or developing tolerance. If these patterns appear, address them early. Substance dependence develops gradually, and early intervention is more effective than waiting until problems are severe.

If you struggle with substance use, seek help. This might mean talking with a healthcare provider, connecting with support groups, or entering treatment. Substance problems rarely improve without intervention. Effective treatments exist; use them.

Creating Sustainable Routines

Isolated healthy choices provide some benefit, but sustainable routines produce lasting results. The goal is setting up patterns that support health without requiring constant decision-making or willpower.

Start with keystone habits: behaviors that naturally support added healthy behaviors. Regular sleep schedules, daily exercise, and planned meals are keystone habits. When these are in place, other healthy choices become easier. Poor sleep undermines exercise motivation and increases craving for unhealthy foods. Regular exercise improves sleep quality and energy levels. Planning meals prevents reliance on less nutritious convenience foods.

Make healthy choices the default choice. If your kitchen has primarily nutritious food, you will eat nutritious food. If you lay out exercise clothes the night before, you are more likely to exercise in the morning. If you keep your phone out of your bedroom, you are more likely to sleep well. Structuring your environment to support healthy choices reduces reliance on willpower.

Stack new habits onto existing routines. After you pour your morning coffee, do five minutes of stretching. After you arrive home from work, change into exercise clothes immediately. After dinner, prepare tomorrow's lunch. Linking new behaviors to set up routines increases consistency.

Track your behaviors to keep awareness. You might use a simple calendar to mark days you exercise, a journal to record sleep and energy levels, or an app to check nutrition. Tracking does not need to be elaborate. The act of recording increases mindfulness and accountability.

Be flexible within structure. Rigid perfectionism about health routines often leads to abandonment when you miss a day or make poor choices. One skipped workout or unhealthy meal does not ruin your health. The pattern over weeks and months decides outcomes. If you miss your routine, simply return to it the next day rather than viewing it as total failure.

Anticipate obstacles and plan accordingly. If you know you will have a busy week, prepare meals in advance. If travel disrupts routines, find how you will support key practices. If holiday gatherings involve less healthy food, decide in advance how you will balance enjoyment with health. Planning prevents obstacles from derailing your routines entirely.

The Road Ahead

Physical health forms the foundation for psychological resilience. Sleep, nutrition, exercise, and stress management directly affect your capacity to manage challenges, regulate emotions, think clearly, and perform effectively. Neglecting these fundamentals undermines everything else you try to do.

Establishing healthy habits requires initial effort but produces compounding returns over time. Well-rested, properly nourished, physically active people have more energy, better moods, clearer thinking, and greater stress resilience than those who neglect these basics. The investment is modest; the returns are large.

Start where you are. You do not need to perfect all health practices simultaneously. Find one or two areas where improvement would have the greatest impact and focus there. As those practices become routine, add others. Gradual sustainable improvement produces better long-term outcomes than trying drastic overnight changes that prove unsustainable.

Chapter 10: Set Realistic Goals

Goals provide direction and motivation. Without clear goals, you drift through circumstances rather than deliberately shaping your life. However, poorly conceived goals create frustration rather than progress. Understanding how to set goals that are challenging yet achievable, specific yet flexible, is essential for sustained success.

Many people set goals that are either too vague to guide action or too rigid to survive contact with reality. Others set unrealistic goals that guarantee failure, or neglect goal setting entirely and then wonder why they achieve little. Effective goal setting is a learnable skill that dramatically improves your capacity to achieve what you want.

The SMART Framework

SMART is an acronym describing qualities of well-formed goals. Goals should be Specific, Measurable, Achievable, Relevant, and Time-bound. This framework helps translate vague aspirations into actionable goals.

Specific means clearly defined. "Be healthier" is vague. "Exercise for 30 minutes five days per week" is specific. Specific goals cut ambiguity about what you are trying to conduct. They answer who, what, where, when, why, and how. The more precisely you define your goal, the clearer your path to achieving it becomes.

Measurable means you can track progress objectively. If you cannot measure whether you are progressing toward a goal, you cannot adjust your approach when needed. Measurable goals include quantifiable criteria:

"Save $5,000," "Read 24 books," "Achieve 3.5 GPA." Measurement provides feedback that allows course correction.

Achievable means realistic given your resources, constraints, and capabilities. Setting impossible goals guarantees failure and damages confidence. Goals should stretch your capabilities without exceeding them. If you currently exercise zero days per week, committing to daily intense workouts is likely unrealistic. Committing to three days per week is challenging but achievable. As you build capacity, you can increase goals.

Relevant means aligned with your broader goals and values. You can achieve a goal and still feel dissatisfied if that goal does not actually matter to you or does not contribute to larger aims. Before committing to a goal, verify that achieving it will meaningfully improve your life or advance priorities that matter to you.

Time-bound means having a deadline. Without a timeframe, goals lack urgency and tend to be perpetually postponed. Deadlines create accountability and help you assess whether your pace is proper. Some goals have natural deadlines imposed by external circumstances. Others require you to set arbitrary but firm deadlines to keep momentum.

Distinguishing Process Goals from Outcome Goals

Outcome goals focus on results: getting a specific job, achieving a certain grade, reaching a target weight. Process goals focus on behaviors: sending three job applications weekly, studying two hours daily, exercising five days per week. Both types have value, but process goals are more directly controllable.

You control process goals directly. You can decide to exercise five days this week and do so. You cannot directly control whether you are hired for a specific job, even if you are qualified. Factors outside your control influence outcomes. Basing your sense of achievement entirely on outcomes means your success depends on things you cannot fully control.

Set outcome goals to define what you are aiming for, then set process goals that lead toward those outcomes. If your outcome goal is securing employment in your field, your process goals might include applying to a certain number of positions weekly, requesting informational interviews monthly, and attending two networking events per month. Following through on process goals does not guarantee the outcome you want, but it maximizes the probability of achieving it.

Process goals build confidence more reliably than outcome goals because you can achieve them through your own actions. Each week you meet your process goals, you show capability and build momentum. This creates positive feedback loops that sustain effort over time.

Breaking Long-Term Goals into Milestones

Large goals can feel overwhelming. A goal that will take years to achieve is too distant to motivate daily action. Breaking long-term goals into intermediate milestones makes them more manageable and provides regular reinforcement.

Milestones are significant progress markers on the path toward your ultimate goal. If your goal is completing a degree, milestones might include completing each semester, finishing prerequisite courses, passing comprehensive exams, or completing your thesis. If your goal is career advancement, milestones might include mastering specific skills, completing projects showing capabilities, or achieving performance evaluations that position you for promotion.

Each milestone should be large enough to feel like real progress but near enough to support motivation. Extremely distant milestones offer little guidance for daily action. Milestones too close together create excessive administrative overhead. Find the proper level of granularity for your situation.

When you achieve milestones, acknowledge your progress. This recognition provides psychological reward that sustains motivation through the next phase. Without celebrating progress, long-term goals become purely effortful with no reinforcement until final completion, which may be years away.

Use milestones to assess whether you are on track. If you consistently miss milestone deadlines, this signals that your timeline is unrealistic, your strategies are ineffective, or unexpected obstacles require adjustment. Early detection through milestone tracking allows course correction before you have invested years in an unworkable approach. *

Tracking Progress Effectively

What gets measured gets managed. Tracking progress provides the information necessary to evaluate whether your approach is working and where adjustments are needed.

Choose tracking methods appropriate to your goals. For behavioral goals, simple habit trackers marking whether you performed target behaviors each day often suffice. For goals involving quantities, spreadsheets tracking relevant numbers work well. For complex projects, tools that break goals into subtasks and track completion provide visibility into progress.

Track regularly enough to detect problems quickly but not so often that tracking becomes burdensome. Daily tracking works well for habit-based goals. Weekly or monthly tracking may be proper for goals where progress is gradual. Find the frequency that provides useful information without excessive effort.

Review your tracking data periodically to show patterns. Are you consistently meeting your targets on some days but not others? Do certain circumstances predict success or failure? What obstacles recur? This pattern recognition enables strategic adjustments rather than vague sense that things are or are not working.

Be honest in your tracking. Self-deception defeats the purpose. If you did not meet your goal, record that fact. Accurate information allows proper response. Inflated tracking makes you think you are progressing when you are not, delaying necessary course corrections.

Adjusting Goals Based on Feedback

Goals should not be set in stone. As you gather information about what is actually involved in achieving them, what obstacles you face, and what your true capabilities and constraints are, you may need to adjust goals.

If you consistently exceed your goals with ease, increase them. Goals that are too easy provide insufficient challenge to promote growth. Push yourself harder when you discover you can manage more.

If you consistently do not meet goals despite genuine effort, either the goals are unrealistic or your strategies are ineffective. Decide which. Are you failing because you set targets that are impossible given your constraints? Then revise the goals to be more realistic. Are you failing because your approach is flawed? Then keep the goal but change your tactics.

Distinguish between goals that should be adjusted and goals where persistence is needed. Some goals take time and sustained effort. Giving up too quickly prevents success. However, continuing to pursue impossible goals wastes resources that could be better applied elsewhere. This judgment call is difficult but examining whether you have genuinely tried multiple approaches or whether progress exists even if it is slower than hoped helps guide the decision.

When circumstances change significantly, reassess all goals. A goal that made sense when set may no longer be relevant after major life changes. Do not continue pursuing goals out of inertia. Verify that goals still align with current priorities and constraints.

Maintaining Motivation

Initial motivation for goals is typically high. You feel excited about the possibility of achievement. Over time, as effort accumulates and novelty fades, motivation wanes. Understanding how to support motivation through the difficult middle period decides success.

Connect goals to meaningful values and outcomes. Goals pursued for external validation or because you think you should want them are difficult to sustain. Goals aligned with your authentic values and desires are intrinsically motivating. When effort feels difficult, reconnecting with why the goal matters to you restores motivation.

Create accountability structures. Tell trusted people about your goals. Report progress regularly. External accountability increases follow-through. Knowing someone will ask about your progress makes you more likely to actually make that progress.

Build supportive environments that make goal pursuit easier. If your goal is exercising regularly, lay out workout clothes the night before, schedule exercise as fixed appointments, and find workout partners. Environmental support reduces reliance on moment-to-moment willpower.

Use implementation intentions: specific plans about when, where, and how you will work toward goals. "I will exercise" is an intention. "I will go to the gym Monday, Wednesday, and Friday at 6:30 AM" is an implementation intention. Specific plans dramatically increase follow-through compared to general intentions.

Celebrate progress regularly rather than waiting for final achievement. Each milestone reached, each week of consistent process goal achievement, each improvement in relevant metrics deserves recognition. Regular celebration provides positive reinforcement that sustains effort.

Anticipate motivational fluctuations. Everyone experiences periods of lower motivation. This is normal. Prepare for them by setting up routines that continue even when motivation is low. Habits and systems reduce dependence on feeling motivated. When motivation returns, you will not have lost significant ground.

Balancing Multiple Goals

You likely have multiple important goals across different life domains: academic or career goals, health goals, relationship goals, financial goals, personal development goals. Pursuing them all simultaneously is challenging. Prioritization and strategic attention allocation are necessary.

Limit the number of major goals you actively pursue simultaneously. Three to five major goals are manageable for most people. More than that and attention becomes too divided to make meaningful progress on any. Choose the goals that matter most currently and defer others until you have capacity.

Some goals synergize; others compete. Goals that synergize support each other. Regular exercise improves energy and mental health, which supports academic or career performance. Building professional skills can simultaneously advance career goals and learning goals. Look for these synergies and use them.

When goals compete for limited time or resources, accept that progress on one may require temporarily reducing emphasis on others. If you are completing a degree while working, your social life may receive less attention during that period. This is not failure; it is realistic resource allocation. The key is making these tradeoffs consciously rather than being frustrated that you cannot maximize everything simultaneously.

Revisit priorities regularly. What deserves emphasis changes as your life circumstances and values evolve. Goals that were central may become less important. New goals may appear. Periodic reassessment ensures you are investing effort in what currently matters most rather than what mattered when you initially set goals.

The Road Ahead

Effective goal setting provides direction, motivation, and framework for measuring progress. Well-formed goals that are specific, measurable, achievable, relevant, and time-bound guide action effectively. Breaking long-term goals into milestones makes them manageable. Tracking progress enables course correction. Adjusting goals based on feedback prevents wasted effort on unworkable approaches.

Goals should serve you, not constrain you. They provide structure and direction, but they are tools, not obligations. When goals no longer serve your aims, revise them. When you achieve goals, set new ones. Goal setting is an ongoing practice, not a one-time activity.

The discipline of setting and pursuing meaningful goals builds confidence in your ability to shape your life deliberately. Each goal achieved proves that you can decide what you want, create plans to get there, and follow through consistently. This capability is foundational to resilience and long-term success.

Chapter 11: Build Resilience Through Experience

Resilience is not an innate trait some people have and others lack. It is a set of capabilities that develop through practice. You become resilient by successfully navigating challenges, extracting lessons from failures, and repeatedly proving to yourself that you can manage difficulty. This chapter addresses how to build resilience deliberately through strategic engagement with challenges.

Many people avoid challenges whenever possible, seeking comfort and minimizing risk. This strategy feels safe but undermines resilience development. Without facing and overcoming difficulties, you never build confidence in your ability to manage them. When inevitable challenges arise, you lack both skills and confidence to manage them effectively. Deliberate challenge-seeking, within proper limits, builds the resilience you will need throughout your life.

Resilience Develops Through Practice

Just as physical strength develops through progressively challenging exercise, psychological resilience develops through encountering and overcoming difficulties. Each challenge successfully navigated builds capability and confidence.

When you face a difficult situation and manage it successfully, several things happen. First, you prove to yourself that you can manage that type of challenge. This increases confidence in your abilities. Second, you develop specific skills and strategies for managing similar situations in the future. Third, your sense of what qualifies as overwhelming expands. What initially seemed impossibly difficult becomes merely challenging after you manage it successfully.

This process is cumulative. Early successes build confidence to try more significant challenges. Those successes further expand your capacity. Over time, you develop broad resilience applicable across diverse situations rather than narrow capacity to manage only specific familiar challenges.

Avoiding all difficulty prevents this developmental process. If you consistently choose the easier path, you never build capability for the harder one. When circumstances force you to face difficulty without having developed resilience through earlier practice, you lack both skills and confidence to manage effectively.

Seeking Appropriate Challenges

The key word is proper. Challenges should stretch your current capabilities without overwhelming them. Challenges far beyond your current capacity produce failure and damage confidence rather than building resilience. Challenges well within your capacity provide insufficient impetus for growth.

Appropriate challenges exist in the zone just beyond your comfort zone: difficult enough to require genuine effort and problem-solving, but not so difficult that success is unlikely even with good effort. This zone varies by individual and by domain. What is appropriately challenging for someone with substantial experience differs from what is proper for a beginner.

Find your current capabilities honestly. What types of challenges do you manage comfortably? What feels overwhelming? Appropriate next challenges fall between these extremes. They should feel somewhat uncomfortable but not impossible.

In academic or professional contexts, this might mean taking on projects slightly more complex than what you have managed previously, volunteering for responsibilities that will stretch your skills, or learning topics next to your current ability. In personal contexts, it might mean starting difficult conversations you have been avoiding, traveling independently to unfamiliar places, or trying activities outside your comfort zone.

You can deliberately seek these challenges rather than waiting for circumstances to impose them. This proactive approach allows you to choose timing, control circumstances to some degree, and prepare adequately. Challenges you choose feel less threatening than challenges imposed on you unexpectedly.

When you successfully manage a challenge that once felt daunting, reflect on what that success demonstrates about your capabilities. Explicitly connect the experience to your growing resilience. This reflection combines learning and builds confidence more effectively than simply moving on to the next challenge without acknowledgment.

Learning from Both Success and Failure

Successes build confidence, but failures often teach more. The question is not whether you will face setbacks—you will—but whether you extract lessons from them that improve future performance.

When things go wrong, your natural response may be self-criticism, discouragement, or avoidance of similar situations in the future. These responses are understandable but counterproductive. More useful is systematic analysis of what happened and what you can learn from it.

Separate controllable factors from uncontrollable ones. Some failures result from genuine errors in judgment, inadequate preparation, or poor execution. These failures hold lessons about what to do differently. Other failures result from circumstances beyond your control: poor timing, factors you could not have predicted, or situations where even best performance would not have succeeded. These failures do not show personal inadequacy.

For failures involving controllable factors, find specifically what you would do differently. Vague self-criticism like "I need to try harder" is less useful than concrete identification of specific improvements: "I need to start assignments earlier," "I need to verify information from multiple sources before making decisions," "I need to practice presentations multiple times before delivering them." Specific lessons can be implemented; general self-criticism cannot.

Recognize that most failures are partial rather than total. Even unsuccessful attempts typically include some elements that worked. Finding what went well alongside what went poorly provides a more correct assessment and prevents you from discarding effective strategies along with ineffective ones.

Failures are data about what does not work, not evidence of personal inadequacy. Reframing failure as information reduces its emotional impact and increases the likelihood that you will persist rather than give up. People who view failures as learning opportunities recover more quickly and ultimately achieve more than people who view failures as confirmation of inability.

Successes also deserve analysis, not just celebration. When something goes well, find why. What strategies worked? What factors contributed to success? Understanding success allows you to replicate it. Too often people attribute success to luck or external factors while blaming themselves for failures. This pattern prevents learning from either. Analyze both successes and failures systematically.

Building Confidence Through Demonstrated Capability

Confidence is not believing you will never fail. It is trust in your ability to manage challenges and recover from setbacks. This confidence develops through accumulated evidence of capability.

Each time you face a difficult situation and manage it successfully, you add to your mental catalog of evidence that you can manage challenges. Over time, this catalog becomes a resource you can draw on when facing new difficulties. You remind yourself: I have managed hard things before. I can manage this.

Keep track of your successes explicitly. When you overcome a challenge, note it. This might be in a journal, a list, or simply a mental inventory you review periodically. When facing new challenges, review this evidence of past capability. This practice counters the tendency to forget successes while remembering failures vividly.

Notice your growth over time. What was difficult six months ago may be routine now. What seemed impossible a year ago may be well within your current capabilities. Recognizing this growth shows that you continue developing, which builds confidence that you can develop further.

Confidence is domain-specific initially. Success in academics builds confidence in your ability to master new material but may not immediately transfer to confidence in social situations or physical challenges. Over time, as you build capability across multiple domains, you develop more general confidence in your ability to figure out whatever you need to.

This generalized confidence is not arrogance. You recognize that you lack ability in many areas. But you trust your ability to learn what you need to know and to manage difficulties when they arise. This trust is the essence of resilience.

Maintaining Long-Term Perspective

Resilience building is a long-term project. Short-term setbacks are inevitable and should not be interpreted as evidence that you are not progressing.

View your development over months and years, not days and weeks. Some periods will feel like backward movement. You will face situations that overwhelm your current capacity. You will make mistakes despite good effort. These experiences are part of growth, not evidence against it.

Long-term perspective helps support motivation during difficult periods. When you are struggling with current challenges, remembering how much you have already grown provides encouragement. The difficulties you manage routinely now were once beyond your capability. Current struggles will likewise become manageable with continued effort.

Accept that resilience is not constant. Everyone has periods of greater and lesser capacity depending on stress levels, life circumstances, health, and other factors. Having a bad week does not erase earlier growth. It simply means you are temporarily running at reduced capacity. This is normal. When circumstances improve, your typical resilience level returns.

Recognize that resilience building is lifelong. You never reach a point where you cannot continue developing. Life will continue presenting new types of challenges requiring new capabilities. The foundation you build now serves you throughout your life, and you can continue building on it indefinitely.

Integrating All Components

This chapter concludes the section on resilience and adaptability. Resilience is not a single skill but an integrated set of capabilities: supporting growth mindset, embracing challenges, building support networks, solving problems systematically, understanding yourself, staying flexible, keeping physical health, setting effective goals, and accumulating experience handling difficulties.

These capabilities reinforce each other. Self-awareness helps you find which challenges are proper for your current level. Problem-solving skills help you navigate those challenges successfully. Support networks provide assistance when challenges exceed your independent capacity. Physical health ensures you have energy and mental clarity to manage stress. Goal setting provides direction and measures progress. Flexibility allows adaptation when initial approaches fail.

You do not need to perfect all these capabilities simultaneously. Progress in any area supports development in others. Start where you are. Find the capabilities that would provide the most value for your current circumstances and develop those first. Success builds momentum that makes developing added capabilities easier.

The strategies described in this section are not theoretical abstractions. They are practical tools that work when applied consistently. Research across psychology, education, organizational behavior, and other fields confirms their effectiveness. Your task is not to debate whether they work but to implement them and adapt them to your specific circumstances.

The Road Ahead

Resilience is the foundation for navigating life effectively. It is not avoiding difficulty but developing capability to manage it. It is not never failing but learning from failures and persisting despite them. It is not superhuman endurance but systematic application of evidence-based strategies for managing challenges.

You build resilience through practice: by seeking proper challenges, learning from both successes and failures, accumulating evidence of your capability, and keeping long-term perspective on your development. This is not passive process that happens to you. It is active practice you engage in deliberately.

The capabilities you develop by building resilience serve you throughout your life. Academic challenges, career obstacles, relationship difficulties, health problems, financial setbacks, and other inevitable difficulties become manageable when you have built strong resilience. The investment you make now in developing these capabilities provides returns for decades to come.

The next sections of this book address specific domains: self-care, financial literacy, digital skills, communication, and career planning. The resilience foundation you have built through this section enables you to apply strategies in those domains more effectively. Resilient people learn faster, persist longer, recover from setbacks more quickly, and ultimately achieve more of what they set out to do. The capabilities you develop now are among the most valuable investments you can make in your future.

Chapter 12: Maintain Optimism and Gratitude

Introduction

Optimism and gratitude are not personality traits you either have or lack. They are cognitive habits that can be developed through deliberate practice. Research in positive psychology consistently shows that people who cultivate these habits experience measurable benefits: lower stress, improved physical health, stronger relationships, greater resilience in the face of adversity, and higher overall life satisfaction. These outcomes are not the result of ignoring problems or pretending difficulties do not exist. They result from training your attention to include what is going well alongside what needs improvement.

Keeping optimism does not mean expecting everything to work out perfectly. Realistic optimism means believing that your actions can influence outcomes, that setbacks are temporary and addressable rather than permanent and defining, and that effort directed toward meaningful goals produces results over time. This orientation toward possibility rather than helplessness directly affects how you respond to challenges. People who maintain realistic optimism persist longer, try more solutions, and recover faster from failures than those who default to pessimism.

Gratitude runs through a different but complementary mechanism. By deliberately attending to what you have rather than fixating on what you lack, gratitude counteracts the natural human tendency toward negativity bias, the well-documented phenomenon where negative experiences receive disproportionate attention compared to positive ones. Regular gratitude practice does not end negative experiences but ensures they do not monopolize your psychological resources.

Why Optimism and Gratitude Matter

Adversity is unavoidable. Failed exams, rejected applications, damaged relationships, financial setbacks, and professional disappointments are standard components of any life. What differs between individuals is not the presence of adversity but the interpretation of it. Optimism provides a framework for interpreting setbacks as temporary, specific, and addressable rather than permanent, pervasive, and personal. This interpretive framework directly affects your emotional response, your willingness to take corrective action, and ultimately the outcomes you achieve.

The physiological benefits of optimism and gratitude are well documented. Chronic pessimism and rumination on negative experiences activate stress responses that, sustained over time, contribute to cardiovascular problems, weakened immune function, sleep disruption, and increased vulnerability to anxiety and depression. Optimism and gratitude practices reduce cortisol levels, lower blood pressure, improve sleep quality, and strengthen immune function. These are not marginal effects. Longitudinal studies show that dispositional optimism is associated with significantly better health outcomes across multiple decades.

Gratitude strengthens relationships by shifting attention toward what others contribute rather than what they do not provide. Expressing appreciation, whether to friends, family members, colleagues, or casual acquaintances, reinforces positive interactions and builds reciprocal goodwill. People who regularly express genuine gratitude report stronger social connections, more supportive relationships, and greater willingness among others to offer help during difficult periods. In practical terms, gratitude functions as social investment that compounds over time.

Optimism and gratitude also improve decision-making under stress. When negative emotions dominate, cognitive processing narrows. You see fewer options, evaluate them less carefully, and default to avoidance or impulsive reactions. Positive emotional states broaden cognitive processing, enabling you to generate more potential solutions, evaluate them more objectively, and select responses aligned with your long-term interests rather than immediate emotional relief. This broader cognitive state is particularly valuable during the high-stress periods when good decisions matter most.

Developing Realistic Optimism

Realistic optimism begins with how you explain events to yourself. Psychologist Martin Seligman's research on explanatory styles finds three dimensions that distinguish optimistic from pessimistic thinking. Permanence concerns whether you view negative events as temporary or permanent. Pervasiveness concerns whether you view negative events as specific to one area or as contaminating everything. Personalization concerns whether you attribute negative events entirely to your own failings or recognize the role of circumstances, other people, and factors beyond your control.

When something goes wrong, notice your automatic interpretation. If you failed a job interview, do you think "I will never get hired" (permanent), "I am bad at everything" (pervasive), and "It is entirely my fault" (personal)? Or do you think "This particular interview did not go well" (temporary), "I need to prepare differently for this type of interview" (specific), and "The position may not have been a strong fit for my current experience" (balanced attribution)? The second pattern is not delusional. It is more correct and more useful. Most negative events are temporary, specific, and caused by multiple factors.

Practice reframing by asking specific questions when you meet setbacks. What did I learn from this experience? What would I do differently next time? What aspects of this situation were within my control and what aspects were not? Is this setback permanent or is it a temporary obstacle? These questions redirect your thinking from helpless rumination toward constructive analysis. The goal is not to minimize genuine problems but to ensure your interpretation of events is correct rather than catastrophically distorted.

Surround yourself with people who model realistic optimism. Social environments powerfully influence cognitive habits. If the people around you consistently interpret events through a pessimistic lens, that interpretation becomes normalized. Seek relationships with people who acknowledge difficulties honestly while keeping confidence in their ability to address them. This does not mean avoiding people who are struggling. It means ensuring your social environment includes people who show the cognitive patterns you want to develop.

Practicing Gratitude Effectively

Gratitude practice is most effective when it is specific, consistent, and genuine. Vague gratitude, being grateful "for everything" or "for life," produces minimal psychological benefit. Specific gratitude, finding particular people, experiences, or circumstances that contributed positively to your day, engages the cognitive processes that produce measurable benefits.

Journaling is the most researched gratitude practice. Writing down three to five specific things you are grateful for each day takes less than five minutes and, when practiced consistently over several weeks, produces measurable improvements in mood, sleep quality, and overall wellbeing. The key is specificity. Rather than writing "I am grateful for my friends," write "I am grateful that Alex called to check on me when I was having a difficult week." Specific entries engage deeper processing and produce stronger effects.

Expressing gratitude directly to others amplifies its benefits for both you and the recipient. A specific, genuine expression of appreciation, whether spoken, written in a message, or communicated through a letter, strengthens the relationship and reinforces your own awareness of positive elements in your life. Research by Martin Seligman found that writing and delivering a detailed gratitude letter to someone who had been particularly kind or influential produced significant increases in happiness that persisted for weeks afterward.

Incorporate gratitude into existing routines rather than treating it as a separate task. Reflecting on one positive aspect of your day during your morning coffee, finding something you appreciated before falling asleep, or mentally noting moments of kindness or competence as they occur throughout the day all build the habit without requiring dedicated time. The goal is to gradually shift your default attentional pattern so that positive experiences receive proper recognition rather than being overlooked in favor of problems and complaints.

Gratitude is particularly valuable during difficult periods. When circumstances are challenging, the deliberate practice of finding what is still good, what support is available, and what progress has been made despite obstacles prevents the cognitive distortion that everything is terrible. This is not denial. It is balanced belief. Acknowledging that a situation is difficult while simultaneously recognizing that you have resources, support, and past evidence of your ability to manage adversity provides a more correct and more functional assessment than focusing exclusively on what is wrong.

The Road Ahead

Optimism and gratitude are skills that strengthen with practice. They do not require you to ignore problems, suppress negative emotions, or keep artificial cheerfulness. They require you to ensure that your interpretation of events is correct rather than catastrophically biased, that your attention includes positive experiences rather than exclusively negative ones, and that you deliberately acknowledge what is working alongside what needs improvement. These cognitive habits directly affect your emotional wellbeing, your physical health, your relationships, and your capacity to respond effectively to the challenges that resilience demands. Developing them is not optional self-help. It is practical maintenance of the psychological foundation on which all other competencies depend.

Section 2: The Importance of Self-Care

Self-care is not luxury but necessity. Sustained performance in any domain requires supporting physical health, mental wellbeing, and emotional stability. Neglecting these fundamentals undermines everything else you try to do.

Many people treat self-care as something to address after handling more urgent priorities. This is backward. Self-care provides the foundation that makes addressing other priorities possible. Without adequate sleep, proper nutrition, regular exercise, and stress management, your capacity to manage challenges deteriorates. Performance declines. Decision quality suffers. Emotional regulation becomes difficult. Physical health problems appear.

The chapters in this section address specific self-care practices that directly affect your functioning: sleep, nutrition, exercise, stress management, mental health maintenance, relationship quality, mindfulness, and boundary setting. These are not abstract wellness concepts but practical requirements for sustained effectiveness.

Research across medicine, psychology, and organizational behavior consistently proves that people who maintain fundamental self-care practices outperform those who neglect them. They experience better health, greater life satisfaction, stronger relationships, and superior professional outcomes. The advantage compounds over time.

The investment needed is modest compared to returns. The practices described in this section require a few hours weekly. This is not optional time that can be eliminated without consequence. It is essential maintenance that prevents far more costly problems later.

Chapter 13: Get Enough Sleep

Sleep is not optional. It is a biological necessity with profound effects on cognitive function, emotional regulation, physical health, and overall performance. Despite this, sleep deprivation is widespread, particularly among young adults. Understanding why sleep matters and how to obtain adequate rest is fundamental to effective self-care.

Why Sleep is Essential

During sleep, your brain combines memories, processes emotions, removes metabolic waste products, and performs essential maintenance. These functions cannot occur during waking hours. Insufficient sleep impairs all of them.

Sleep enhances learning and memory. Information you meet during the day is initially stored in temporary buffers. During sleep, particularly during deep sleep stages, this information is transferred to long-term storage and integrated with existing knowledge. This is why studying before sleep improves retention more than studying followed by continued waking activity. It also explains why sleep deprivation impairs learning even if you spend added hours trying to study.

Emotional regulation depends heavily on adequate sleep. Sleep deprivation particularly affects the prefrontal cortex, which regulates emotional responses. Without sufficient sleep, you become more reactive to negative stimuli, less able to regulate emotional responses, and more prone to anxiety and irritability. Minor frustrations feel overwhelming. Normal social interactions feel stressful. Decision-making becomes more impulsive and less rational.

Physical health requires sleep for multiple processes. Sleep supports immune function; sleep-deprived people are significantly more susceptible to infection. Sleep regulates hormones affecting appetite, metabolism, and growth. It enables tissue repair and muscle recovery. Chronic sleep deprivation increases risk of obesity, diabetes, cardiovascular disease, and other serious health problems.

Sleep affects cardiovascular health directly. During sleep, heart rate and blood pressure decrease, allowing the cardiovascular system to recover from daytime stress. Chronic sleep deprivation keeps these elevated, contributing to hypertension and increased cardiovascular disease risk.

Performance across all domains declines with insufficient sleep. Reaction times slow. Attention lapses. Judgment deteriorates. Problem-solving capability decreases. Creative thinking suffers. These effects accumulate with successive nights of inadequate sleep. People become progressively less capable while often staying unaware of how impaired they have become.

Sleep Requirements

Adults need seven to nine hours of sleep nightly. Individual needs vary within this range, but very few people function optimally on less than seven hours despite commonly believing they do. The research on this is clear: people who sleep less than seven hours show measurable cognitive and physical impairments even when they subjectively feel they are functioning well.

Teenagers and young adults often need closer to nine hours due to ongoing development. This conflicts with academic and social schedules that encourage late nights and early mornings. The biological preference for later sleep times during adolescence combined with early school start times creates chronic sleep deprivation for many students.

Sleep debt accumulates. If you consistently sleep six hours nightly when you need eight, you accumulate two hours of sleep debt daily. This debt cannot be eliminated by occasional extended sleep on weekends. While extra weekend sleep provides some recovery, it does not fully compensate for chronic weekday deprivation. The effects of accumulated sleep debt include increased disease risk, impaired cognitive function, and emotional dysregulation.

Quality matters as much as quantity. Sleep has distinct stages, each serving different functions. Deep sleep is particularly important for physical restoration and memory consolidation. REM sleep supports emotional processing and certain types of learning. Factors that disrupt sleep architecture, such as alcohol, certain medications, or sleep disorders, reduce sleep quality even if total sleep duration appears adequate.

Creating Effective Sleep Habits

Consistent sleep and wake times are foundational. Your circadian rhythm, the biological clock regulating sleep-wake cycles, functions best with regularity. Going to bed and waking at consistent times, including weekends, strengthens this rhythm and makes falling asleep and waking easier.

Many people sleep less during the week and try to compensate on weekends. This creates "social jet lag," shifting the circadian rhythm back and forth weekly. This makes falling asleep on Sunday night difficult and contributes to impaired functioning early in the week. Maintaining consistent timing, even on weekends, prevents this problem.

Your sleep environment significantly affects sleep quality. Bedrooms should be dark, quiet, and cool. Light suppresses melatonin production, the hormone that promotes sleep. Even small amounts of light from electronics or external sources can disrupt sleep. Use blackout curtains or eye masks if needed.

Noise disrupts sleep even when you do not consciously wake. If you live in a noisy environment, consider white noise machines or earplugs to mask disruptive sounds.

Temperature affects sleep quality substantially. Most people sleep best in rooms between 60 and 67 degrees Fahrenheit. Your core body temperature needs to drop to start sleep. Excessively warm rooms interfere with this process.

Avoid screens for at least one hour before bed. The blue wavelength light emitted by phones, tablets, computers, and televisions suppresses melatonin production, making sleep onset more difficult. Additionally, engaging content keeps your mind active when you should be winding down. If you must use screens near bedtime, use blue light filtering features and choose calming rather than stimulating content.

Develop a pre-sleep routine that signals your body that sleep is approaching. This might include reading, light stretching, meditation, or other relaxing activities. Consistency matters; performing the same activities before bed each night conditions your body to prepare for sleep.

Avoid caffeine for at least six hours before bed. Caffeine has a half-life of approximately five to six hours, meaning that six hours after consumption, half is still in your system. Afternoon coffee or evening tea can interfere with sleep even if you successfully fall asleep initially, as caffeine reduces deep sleep quality.

Avoid alcohol near bedtime. While alcohol may help you fall asleep initially, it significantly disrupts sleep architecture. It reduces REM sleep and causes more fragmented, lighter sleep later in the night. You may spend more time in bed but obtain less restorative sleep.

Exercise regularly but avoid intense exercise within three hours of bedtime. Regular physical activity improves sleep quality, but exercising too close to bedtime can interfere with sleep onset due to elevated body temperature and increased alertness. Morning or afternoon exercise provides sleep benefits without this interference.

If you cannot fall asleep within 20 minutes, get up and do something quiet and non-stimulating until you feel sleepy. Lying awake in bed conditions your brain to associate bed with wakefulness rather than sleep. Breaking this association prevents the problem from worsening.

Addressing Common Sleep Problems

Insomnia, difficulty falling asleep or staying asleep, affects many people periodically. Occasional insomnia related to stress or schedule changes typically resolves when circumstances normalize. Chronic insomnia lasting more than three months calls for professional evaluation.

For transient insomnia, focus on sleep hygiene: consistent schedule, proper environment, avoiding stimulants, managing stress. If anxiety about not sleeping perpetuates the problem, remind yourself that occasional poor sleep is normal and does not cause lasting harm. The anxiety often interferes with sleep more than the actual sleep loss.

Sleep disorders such as sleep apnea, restless leg syndrome, or circadian rhythm disorders require medical treatment. If you consistently feel unrefreshed despite apparently adequate sleep duration, snore loudly, experience leg movements or sensations that disrupt sleep, or have extreme difficulty keeping proper sleep timing, consult a healthcare provider. These conditions are treatable but require diagnosis.

Some medications, both prescription and over the counter, affect sleep. If you experience sleep changes after starting new medications, discuss this with your healthcare provider. Do not stop prescribed medications without medical guidance but be aware that medications may contribute to sleep problems.

The Costs of Sleep Deprivation

Sleep deprivation is not benign. The effects extend beyond feeling tired. Cognitive impairment from 24 hours without sleep is comparable to having a blood alcohol content of 0.10 percent, above the legal limit for driving in most jurisdictions. People with chronic partial sleep deprivation accumulate similar impairments.

Driving while sleep-deprived is dangerous. Drowsy driving causes a substantial proportion of fatal crashes. If you feel sleepy while driving, pull over safely and rest. The few minutes of lost time are vastly preferable to the consequences of driving while impaired.

Academic and professional performance suffer from insufficient sleep. Students who sleep adequately perform better academically than those who sacrifice sleep to study more. Workers who are well-rested make better decisions, produce higher quality work, and have fewer accidents than those who are sleep deprived. The belief that you can support performance through sheer effort while neglecting sleep is incorrect.

Long-term health consequences of chronic sleep deprivation are serious. Increased cardiovascular disease risk, higher obesity rates, impaired immune function, and increased susceptibility to mental health problems all correlate with insufficient sleep. These are not minor effects; they significantly affect longevity and quality of life.

Prioritizing Sleep

Despite knowing that sleep is important, many people consistently deprioritize it. This typically results from viewing sleep as flexible time that can be reduced when other demands arise. This perspective is counterproductive.

Sleep is not wasted time but essential maintenance that enables everything else. The hours you invest in adequate sleep produce returns in improved function during waking hours. You do more when well-rested than when trying to extend productive time by reducing sleep.

Treating sleep as a non-negotiable priority, like any other essential activity, helps support consistent sleep habits. Schedule sleep just as you schedule classes, work, or other commitments. Protect this time from encroachment by other activities.

This requires saying no to activities that would interfere with adequate sleep. Late-night social activities, extended work or study sessions, or entertainment can all be enjoyable, but not when they consistently compromise sleep. Make trade-offs consciously rather than defaulting to sleep sacrifice.

The Road Ahead

Sleep is fundamental to physical health, mental functioning, and emotional wellbeing. Adequate sleep improves learning, memory, emotional regulation, immune function, cardiovascular health, and overall performance. Sleep deprivation impairs all of these domains significantly.

Most adults need seven to nine hours of sleep nightly. Maintaining consistent sleep and wake times, creating an environment conducive to sleep, avoiding substances and activities that interfere with sleep, and developing a consistent pre-sleep routine all support good sleep quality.

Prioritizing sleep means treating it as essential rather than optional. The investment of adequate time in sleep produces substantial returns in improved function during waking hours. This is not self-indulgence but practical necessity.

Chapter 14: Eating a Healthy Diet

Nutrition directly affects energy levels, cognitive function, mood, immune response, and long-term health. What you eat matters. The standard modern diet, heavy in processed foods and lacking in essential nutrients, contributes to obesity, chronic disease, and suboptimal functioning. Understanding basic nutrition principles and implementing them consistently improves both immediate performance and long-term health outcomes.

Nutrition Fundamentals

Your body needs macronutrients (carbohydrates, proteins, and fats) for energy and various metabolic functions, plus micronutrients (vitamins and minerals) that support specific biological processes. A balanced diet provides all of these in proper proportions.

Carbohydrates provide readily available energy. They break down into glucose, which fuels brain function and physical activity. Not all carbohydrates are equivalent. Complex carbohydrates from whole grains, vegetables, and legumes provide sustained energy and fiber. Simple carbohydrates from added sugars provide quick energy followed by crashes, contributing to energy instability and health problems when consumed excessively.

Proteins support tissue building and repair, immune function, and various metabolic processes. Complete proteins holding all essential amino acids come primarily from animal sources (meat, fish, eggs, dairy) and certain plant combinations (rice and beans, for example). Adequate protein intake is particularly important during growth periods and when physically active.

Fats are essential for hormone production, nutrient absorption, brain function, and cellular structure. Despite historical vilification of dietary fat, research shows that the type of fat matters more than total fat consumption. Unsaturated fats from plant oils, nuts, seeds, and fish support health. Saturated fats from animal products can be consumed in moderation. Trans fats from partially hydrogenated oils should be avoided entirely.

Vitamins and minerals enable countless biological processes. Deficiencies produce specific symptoms ranging from fatigue to immune dysfunction to cognitive impairment. A varied diet rich in fruits, vegetables, whole grains, and protein sources typically provides adequate micronutrients without requiring supplementation for most people.

Fiber aids digestion, regulates blood sugar, and supports cardiovascular health. Most people consume insufficient fiber. Increasing consumption of fruits, vegetables, whole grains, and legumes addresses this.

Water is essential for virtually every bodily function. Adequate hydration supports physical performance, cognitive function, and overall health. Aim for approximately half your body weight in ounces of water daily, more if you exercise heavily or live in hot climates.

Practical Nutrition Guidelines

Focus on whole, minimally processed foods. These provide nutrients in forms your body evolved to use efficiently. Processed foods often have excessive sodium, added sugars, and unhealthy fats while being stripped of fiber and micronutrients. Base your diet on vegetables, fruits, whole grains, legumes, nuts, seeds, lean proteins, and healthy fats.

Include vegetables at most meals. Aim for variety in types and colors, as different vegetables provide different nutrients. Both cooked and raw vegetables have value. Prepare them in ways you find appealing, so you actually eat them consistently.

Choose whole grains over refined grains. Brown rice, quinoa, oats, whole wheat bread, and similar options provide more nutrients and fiber than white rice, white bread, and other refined grain products. This improves satiety and blood sugar stability.

Include adequate protein distributed throughout the day. This supports muscle maintenance, satiety, and stable energy. Vary protein sources: fish, poultry, lean meat, eggs, dairy, legumes, tofu, and nuts all contribute.

Limit added sugars. Natural sugars in whole fruits come with fiber and nutrients that moderate blood sugar impact. Added sugars in processed foods and beverages provide calories without nutritional value and contribute to many health problems when consumed excessively. Read labels, sugar hides in unexpected products including bread, sauces, and savory foods.

Minimize processed and fast foods. While convenient, these typically provide poor nutrition per calorie. Occasional consumption is fine, but basing your diet on these foods leads to poor nutrition and health problems.

Pay attention to portion sizes. Even healthy foods contribute to weight gain when consumed in excessive quantities. Use smaller plates, serve proper portions, and pay attention to hunger and fullness signals rather than eating everything served.

Eat mindfully rather than while distracted. Eating while watching television, working, or using phones leads to consuming more food with less satisfaction. Paying attention to what you eat helps you recognize proper stopping points.

Meal Planning and Preparation

Having nutritious food readily available makes healthy eating far easier. When you are hungry and have no prepared options, you default to whatever is most convenient, which is typically less nutritious.

Plan meals in advance. This need not be elaborate. Simply deciding what you will eat for the next few days prevents decision paralysis when hungry and ensures you have needed ingredients available.

Prepare food in batches when you have time. Cooking larger quantities and portioning for later meals offers convenient healthy options without repeated cooking time. Grains, proteins, and vegetables can all be prepared in advance.

Keep healthy snacks accessible. When you want a snack, you eat whatever is available. Having fruits, vegetables, nuts, yogurt, or other nutritious options readily accessible makes choosing them natural.

Learn basic cooking skills. You do not need to become a chef but knowing how to prepare simple meals from whole ingredients gives you control over what you eat. This is cheaper and healthier than relying on prepared foods or restaurants.

Common Nutrition Mistakes

Skipping meals, particularly breakfast, often leads to excessive hunger later and poor food choices. Regular meals support stable blood sugar and energy. If you struggle to eat breakfast, start with something small and simple.

Restrictive dieting typically backfires. Severe calorie restriction, elimination of entire food groups without medical reason, or rigid food rules often lead to preoccupation with food, binge eating, and disordered eating patterns. Focus on eating nutritious foods in proper amounts rather than on restriction.

Drinking calories from soda, juice, sweetened coffee drinks, and alcohol adds large calories without contributing to satiety. These calories are easy to consume in excess. Water and unsweetened beverages should be your primary fluids.

Eating too quickly prevents recognition of fullness. It takes approximately 20 minutes for satiety signals to register. Eating rapidly leads to consuming more food than needed. Slow down; you will enjoy food more and eat proper amounts.

Emotional eating uses food to manage uncomfortable emotions rather than to satisfy hunger. This is common but problematic. Food provides temporary distraction but does not address underlying issues. Developing other coping strategies reduces reliance on eating for emotional regulation.

Nutrition for Specific Situations

Athletic activity increases caloric and nutrient needs. If you exercise regularly, you need adequate fuel. Insufficient nutrition impairs both performance and recovery. Timing matters: eating carbohydrates before exercise provides energy, while consuming protein after exercise supports recovery.

During high-stress periods, maintaining good nutrition becomes both harder and more important. Stress increases cortisol, which affects appetite and food choices. Many people either lose appetite or crave comfort foods. Conscious effort to keep regular, nutritious meals supports stress management.

Budget constraints affect food choices but do not prevent healthy eating. Dried beans, lentils, rice, oats, seasonal produce, eggs, and frozen vegetables provide good nutrition inexpensively. Cooking from whole ingredients is cheaper than buying processed foods or eating out.

Social situations involving food can make healthy eating challenging. You can enjoy social occasions while making reasonable choices. Eat normally before events so you are not ravenously hungry. At events, choose smaller portions or balance indulgent options with healthier ones. Most importantly, do not attach moral judgment to food choices at social occasions. Flexibility is part of sustainable healthy eating.

Building Sustainable Habits

Sustainable nutrition changes happen gradually. Attempting to overhaul your entire diet overnight rarely works. Find one or two changes you can implement consistently. After these become routine, add others.

Make your environment support your goals. Keep healthy foods visible and accessible. Keep less healthy options out of sight or out of your home entirely. You eat what is convenient.

Expect imperfection. You will eat foods you intended to avoid. You will skip meal preparation occasionally. This is normal. The pattern over weeks and months matters, not individual choices. Get back on track with your next meal rather than viewing deviation as failure.

Track your intake periodically to increase awareness. You do not need to count calories permanently but recording what you eat for a week or two often reveals patterns you were unaware of. This awareness enables more informed choices.

The Road Ahead

Nutrition affects every aspect of your functioning. A diet based on whole foods, with adequate protein, complex carbohydrates, healthy fats, and abundant fruits and vegetables provides the foundation for best health and performance. Limiting processed foods, added sugars, and excessive portions prevents common nutrition-related health problems.

Good nutrition does not require perfection or complicated rules. It requires consistent application of basic principles: eat mostly whole foods, include variety, pay attention to portions, and keep regular meals. These habits, implemented consistently, produce substantial improvements in energy, mental clarity, physical health, and long-term disease risk.

Chapter 15: Exercise Regularly

Regular physical activity is essential for health, functioning, and wellbeing. Exercise provides benefits extending far beyond physical fitness, including improved mood, reduced anxiety and depression, enhanced cognitive function, better sleep quality, and increased resilience to stress. Despite these benefits, most people are insufficiently active. Understanding why exercise matters and how to keep consistent activity makes incorporating it into your life more possible.

Why Exercise Matters

Physical activity affects virtually every system in your body. Cardiovascular exercise strengthens your heart, improves circulation, and enhances your body's ability to use oxygen efficiently. Strength training builds muscle mass, keeps bone density, and supports metabolic health. Both forms reduce chronic disease risk substantially.

Exercise improves mental health through multiple mechanisms. Physical activity stimulates release of endorphins and other neurotransmitters that elevate mood. It reduces stress hormones like cortisol. It provides distraction from rumination. Regular exercisers experience lower rates of depression and anxiety than sedentary people, and exercise is an effective treatment for mild to moderate depression.

Cognitive benefits of exercise are large. Physical activity improves attention, memory, processing speed, and executive function. These effects appear immediately after single exercise sessions and compound with regular activity. Students who exercise regularly perform better academically than comparably intelligent sedentary students. Workers who exercise make better decisions and produce higher quality work.

Sleep quality improves with regular exercise. Physically active people fall asleep faster, sleep more deeply, and wake feeling more rested than inactive people. The effect is reliable enough that exercise is recommended as treatment for insomnia.

Stress resilience increases with regular exercise. Physical activity provides a controlled stressor that trains your stress response systems. This makes you more resilient to other stressors. Physically active people report less perceived stress and recover from stressful events more quickly than inactive people.

Long-term health effects are profound. Regular exercise reduces risk of heart disease, stroke, type 2 diabetes, certain cancers, and many other chronic diseases. It extends lifespan and supports functional ability longer. The size of these effects rivals medication interventions for many conditions.

Exercise Requirements

Current recommendations call for at least 150 minutes of moderate-intensity aerobic activity or 75 minutes of vigorous-intensity aerobic activity weekly, plus strength training at least twice weekly targeting major muscle groups. This translates to 30 minutes of moderate activity five days per week or 25 minutes of vigorous activity three days per week, plus two strength sessions.

Moderate-intensity activity includes brisk walking, recreational swimming, doubles tennis, active recreational activities, and similar efforts where you can talk but not sing comfortably. Your heart rate increases noticeably but you are not gasping for breath.

Vigorous-intensity activity includes running, swimming laps, singles tennis, cycling at higher speeds, and similar efforts where maintaining conversation is difficult. Your heart rate increases substantially, and you breathe hard.

Both intensity levels provide health benefits. Vigorous activity provides similar benefits in less time. Moderate activity is easier to sustain for longer periods and may be more proper if you are beginning an exercise program.

Strength training involves working major muscle groups: legs, hips, back, chest, shoulders, and arms. This might include weight lifting, resistance band exercises, bodyweight exercises (pushups, squats, etc.), or activities like rock climbing. Strength training keeps muscle mass, supports bone density, improves metabolism, and reduces injury risk. It is particularly important as you age, when muscle mass naturally declines without resistance training.

More activity provides added benefits up to a point. Current evidence suggests best health benefits occur around 300 minutes of moderate activity weekly, roughly double the minimum recommendation. Beyond this, added health benefits are modest. For most people, meeting minimum recommendations provides substantial benefit.

Getting Started

If you currently do little physical activity, start where you are. Any increase in activity provides benefits. Walking 10 minutes daily is dramatically better than staying sedentary. From this baseline, gradually increase duration and intensity as your capacity improves.

Choose activities you genuinely enjoy or at least tolerate. You are far more likely to keep exercise you find pleasant than exercise you view as punishment. Experiment with different activities to find what suits you. Some people thrive in group fitness classes; others prefer solitary activities. Some enjoy competitive sports; others prefer individual challenges.

Make exercise convenient. Reduce barriers to physical activity. Choose gyms close to home or work. Exercise at times that fit your schedule reliably. Keep workout clothes and equipment readily accessible. The easier you make exercise, the more likely you are to do it consistently.

Schedule exercise as you schedule other commitments. Waiting to exercise when you feel like it or when time happens to be available typically means not exercising. Treat exercise appointments as seriously as work or academic obligations.

Start with achievable goals. Committing to daily intense workouts when you currently exercise zero days per week sets yourself up for failure. Commit to what you can realistically support, then increase gradually as exercise becomes habitual.

Maintaining Consistency

The most effective exercise program is the one you actually follow consistently. Elaborate best programs you do not support provide no benefit. Simple programs you follow consistently produce substantial results.

Build exercise into your routine rather than treating it as optional. Link it to other established habits: exercise after waking, after work, or before dinner. Consistency in timing makes exercise automatic rather than requiring repeated decisions.

Prepare the night before. Lay out workout clothes. Pack your gym bag. Cut morning decisions that could derail exercise.

Find accountability mechanisms. Exercise with friends or join group activities. Use apps that track activity. Tell others about your goals. External accountability increases follow-through.

Vary your activities to prevent boredom and reduce overuse injury risk. Cross-training, using different activities on different days, allows specific muscle groups to recover while supporting overall fitness. It also keeps exercise interesting.

Accept that motivation fluctuates. You will not always feel like exercising. Exercise anyway. Waiting until you feel motivated means exercising inconsistently. Habits and systems reduce dependence on moment-to-moment motivation.

When you miss scheduled exercise, return to your routine the next day rather than viewing it as total failure. Occasional missed sessions do not ruin fitness. Allowing one missed session to derail consistent habits does.

Overcoming Common Obstacles

Time constraints are the most commonly cited barrier. Most people can find 30 minutes daily if they prioritize it. Exercise does not require hour-long gym sessions. Three 10-minute walks distributed throughout the day provide similar benefits to one 30-minute walk.

Lack of access to facilities is often cited as a barrier. Many effective exercises require no equipment: walking, running, bodyweight exercises, and stretching need only space and time. Online videos provide guided workouts requiring minimal equipment.

Self-consciousness about ability or appearance prevents some people from exercising in public spaces. This is understandable but counterproductive. Most people at gyms or fitness classes focus on their own workouts, not on judging others. If public exercise feels impossible, start with home-based activities until confidence develops.

Earlier negative experiences with exercise often stem from excessive intensity or activities you genuinely disliked. Exercise should challenge you but not feel like torture. If you hated running, do not run. Find activities that feel sustainable.

Physical limitations require modification but rarely prevent all exercise. Most conditions accommodate some form of physical activity. Consult healthcare providers about proper activities if you have health concerns, but do not assume limitations prevent all exercise.

Exercise and Mental Health

Regular exercise is among the most effective interventions for mild to moderate depression and anxiety. The effect size is comparable to medication for many people. Exercise is not a complete substitute for professional treatment when needed, but it is a powerful tool that should be part of comprehensive mental health management.

The mental health benefits of exercise occur through multiple pathways. Physical activity alters neurotransmitter levels, reduces inflammation, improves stress hormone regulation, enhances self-efficacy, provides structure and routine, and offers distraction from rumination.

For maximum mental health benefit, aim for consistency over intensity. Regular moderate exercise provides more mental health benefit than sporadic intense exercise. The discipline of supporting a routine itself builds confidence and sense of control.

Outdoor exercise may provide added mental health benefits beyond indoor exercise. Natural environments reduce rumination and improve mood. If possible, include some outdoor physical activity in your routine.

The Road Ahead

Regular physical activity is essential for physical health, mental wellbeing, cognitive function, and overall quality of life. The benefits extend far beyond fitness or appearance, affecting virtually every aspect of functioning.

Meeting minimum recommendations of 150 minutes of moderate-intensity aerobic activity plus strength training twice weekly provides substantial health benefits. This requires modest time investment with enormous returns.

The key to gaining these benefits is consistency. Find activities you can keep long-term, build them into your routine, and protect that time from competing demands. The discipline of regular exercise compounds over time, producing effects that dramatically improve both immediate functioning and long-term health outcomes.

Chapter 16: Manage Stress

Stress is inevitable. How you manage it decides whether it enhances or impairs your performance and wellbeing. Acute stress can improve focus and motivate action. Chronic unmanaged stress damages physical health, impairs cognitive function, and undermines emotional stability. Developing effective stress management strategies is essential for sustained functioning.

Understanding Stress

Stress is your body's response to demands or threats. When you perceive a challenge, your nervous system activates the fight-or-flight response: heart rate increases, muscles tense, breathing quickens, and stress hormones flood your system. This response evolved to manage immediate physical threats. It mobilizes resources for quick action.

Modern stressors rarely require physical action but trigger the same response. Academic deadlines, work pressures, relationship conflicts, and financial concerns all activate stress responses designed for brief physical emergencies. When stressors are chronic and the stress response stays activated, problems appear.

Chronic stress affects physical health substantially. Elevated stress hormones contribute to hypertension, impaired immune function, digestive problems, and increased inflammation. These effects accumulate over time, increasing risk of serious health conditions including cardiovascular disease.

Cognitive function suffers under chronic stress. The prefrontal cortex, responsible for complex thinking and emotional regulation, functions poorly when stress hormones stay elevated. Memory, attention, and decision-making all deteriorate. Problems seem overwhelming when cognitive resources are impaired.

Emotional regulation becomes difficult under sustained stress. You become more reactive, less patient, and less capable of managing emotional responses. Minor frustrations feel like major problems. Relationships suffer as irritability and reduced empathy make positive interactions harder.

Identifying Your Stress Signals

Stress manifests differently for different people. Some experience primarily physical symptoms: headaches, muscle tension, stomach upset, or fatigue. Others notice emotional symptoms: irritability, anxiety, feeling overwhelmed, or mood swings. Still others see behavioral changes: disrupted sleep, appetite changes, social withdrawal, or increased substance use.

Learn to recognize your stress signals early. When you notice these signs before stress becomes severe, you can implement management strategies before function is significantly impaired. Keep track of what situations trigger stress responses and what symptoms you experience.

Distinguish between acute and chronic stress. Acute stress related to specific events typically resolves when circumstances change. Chronic stress persists over weeks or months. Chronic stress requires more systematic intervention than acute stress.

Physical Stress Management Techniques

Physical activity is among the most effective stress management tools. Exercise reduces stress hormones, increases endorphins, provides distraction from stressors, and improves overall stress resilience. Even brief activity—a ten-minute walk, a few minutes of stretching—can shift your physiological state and improve mood.

Deep breathing activates the parasympathetic nervous system, countering the stress response. When stressed, breathing becomes rapid and shallow. Deliberately slowing and deepening your breath signals your nervous system that the threat has passed. Practice breathing slowly through your nose, expanding your abdomen, holding briefly, then exhaling slowly. Several cycles of deep breathing measurably reduce physiological stress.

Progressive muscle relaxation systematically reduces physical tension. Tense individual muscle groups for five seconds, then release and notice the sensation of relaxation. Work through major muscle groups: hands, arms, shoulders, face, chest, abdomen, legs, feet. This practice both reduces immediate tension and trains awareness of muscle tension so you can address it earlier.

Adequate sleep is essential for stress management. Sleep deprivation amplifies stress responses and impairs coping capacity. Prioritize sleep even when—especially when—stress is high. Sacrificing sleep to address stressors typically worsens rather than improves the situation.

Limit caffeine and alcohol when stressed. Caffeine increases physiological arousal, potentially intensifying anxiety. Alcohol may provide temporary relaxation but disrupts sleep and emotional regulation. Neither substance addresses underlying stress and both can worsen stress management.

Cognitive Stress Management Techniques

Cognitive reappraisal involves changing how you think about stressful situations. Not all stress comes from circumstances themselves but from how you interpret them. Viewing challenges as opportunities for growth rather than threats reduces stress. Focusing on what you can control rather than what you cannot reduces feelings of helplessness.

Problem-focused coping addresses stressors directly. When stress stems from specific problems, solving those problems cuts the stress. Find what you can do to improve the situation. Break problems into manageable steps. Take action on what you can control.

Emotion-focused coping helps when stressors cannot be eliminated. This involves managing your emotional response to situations you cannot change. Acceptance does not mean liking the situation but acknowledging reality rather than fighting against what you cannot alter.

Avoid catastrophizing. When stressed, people often imagine worst-case scenarios and treat them as likely outcomes. This amplifies stress without providing useful information. Challenge catastrophic thinking by considering more realistic possibilities and reminding yourself of past situations where feared outcomes did not materialize.

Practice self-compassion. People often add to stress by criticizing themselves harshly when struggling. Treat yourself with the kindness you would offer a friend in similar circumstances. Acknowledge difficulty without self-condemnation.

Social Support for Stress Management

Social connection buffers against stress. Talking with trusted friends or family about stressors provides emotional validation and often new perspectives on problems. Social isolation increases stress and reduces coping capacity.

Be specific when seeking support. Some situations call for emotional support: someone to listen without judgment and acknowledge your feelings. Other situations call for practical help: help with tasks or advice about approaches. Different people provide different types of support. Choose who to talk with based on what you need.

Support works both ways. Providing support to others can be meaningful and reduces your own stress. Helping others provides perspective on your own difficulties and creates positive connections that buffer against stress.

Professional support may be necessary for severe or chronic stress. If stress significantly impairs functioning, causes persistent physical symptoms, leads to substance abuse as coping mechanism, or triggers thoughts of self-harm, seek help from a mental health professional. There is no benefit in struggling alone with serious stress when effective treatments exist.

Lifestyle Factors in Stress Management

Regular enjoyable activities provide recovery from work demands and support wellbeing. Hobbies, creative pursuits, time in nature, and leisure activities should not be luxuries reserved for when everything else is complete. They are essential maintenance that prevents stress accumulation.

Maintain boundaries between work and personal time. Constant availability increases stress and prevents recovery. Establish periods when you disconnect from work communication. Protect personal time from work encroachment.

Limit exposure to stressors you can control. You cannot end all stress, but you can reduce exposure to unnecessary stressors. This might mean limiting news consumption if current events cause distress, setting boundaries with people who consistently increase stress, or simplifying aspects of life that create complexity without adding value.

Develop realistic expectations. Perfectionism and unrealistic standards create constant stress as you perpetually fall short of impossible goals. Excellence is achievable; perfection is not. Accepting that some outcomes will be good enough rather than best reduces stress substantially.

Time Management and Stress

Much stress stems from feeling overwhelmed by competing demands. Effective time management reduces this stress even when total workload does not change.

Prioritize ruthlessly. Not everything can be equally important. Find what truly matters and distribute time accordingly. Be willing to let less important things go.

Break large projects into smaller tasks. Overwhelming projects become manageable when divided into specific actionable steps. This also provides regular sense of progress, which reduces stress.

Use schedules and to-do lists to externalize memory demands. Trying to remember everything creates background stress. Writing tasks down frees mental resources and ensures nothing is forgotten.

Build buffer time into schedules. Back-to-back commitments with no margin for delays or complications creates constant stress. Realistic scheduling includes cushions for unexpected issues.

Learn to say no. Taking on more than you can manage guarantees stress. Declining requests that exceed your capacity is necessary boundary-setting, not selfishness.

Building Long-Term Stress Resilience

Stress resilience develops through regular self-care practices, not just through crisis management. Physical fitness, adequate sleep, good nutrition, and regular relaxation practices create reserve capacity that allows you to manage acute stressors more effectively.

Develop multiple coping strategies rather than relying on a single approach. What works in one situation may not work in another. Having a repertoire of techniques provides flexibility to address different stressors appropriately.

View stress as information about demands exceeding current capacity. Rather than simply trying to tolerate escalating stress, use it as signal that something needs to change: reduce demands, increase resources, or improve efficiency.

Remember that stress management is ongoing practice, not a one-time fix. New stressors appear continuously. The skills you develop apply across situations. Each time you successfully manage stress, you build confidence in your ability to manage future challenges.

The Road Ahead

Stress is inevitable but manageable. While you cannot cut all stressors, you can develop strategies that reduce their impact and keep your functioning during difficult periods.

Effective stress management combines multiple approaches: physical techniques like exercise and breathing, cognitive strategies like reappraisal, social support, proper problem-solving, and lifestyle practices that support baseline resilience. Different situations call for different strategies.

The investment in developing stress management skills pays large dividends. People who manage stress effectively experience better physical health, superior cognitive function, more stable moods, and greater life satisfaction than those who allow stress to accumulate unchecked. These skills improve with practice and serve you throughout your life.

Chapter 17: Prioritize Mental Health

Mental health is as important as physical health and requires similar attention. Mental health problems are common, treatable, and nothing to be ashamed of. Recognizing signs of mental health difficulties, understanding when to seek help, and knowing what treatments exist enables you to address problems before they become severe.

Understanding Mental Health

Mental health exists on a continuum. Everyone experiences occasional sadness, anxiety, or stress. These are normal responses to challenging circumstances. Mental health problems occur when symptoms become severe enough to impair functioning, persist despite changing circumstances, or cause significant distress.

Common mental health conditions include depression, anxiety disorders, eating disorders, substance use disorders, and trauma-related conditions. These are medical conditions with biological, psychological, and social components. They are not character flaws or personal weaknesses.

Mental health conditions affect approximately one in five adults annually. Many people experiencing mental health problems do not seek treatment, often due to stigma or lack of awareness that their symptoms are treatable. This delay allows problems to worsen and become more difficult to address.

Mental health significantly affects physical health. Depression increases risk of cardiovascular disease. Anxiety worsens various physical conditions. Untreated mental health problems often lead to substance abuse as attempts at self-medication. The division between mental and physical health is artificial; they are deeply interconnected.

Recognizing Warning Signs

Depression involves persistent low mood, loss of interest in activities, changes in sleep or appetite, fatigue, difficulty concentrating, feelings of worthlessness, and sometimes thoughts of death or suicide. Everyone feels sad sometimes. Depression is distinguished by duration (lasting at least two weeks), severity (significantly affecting function), and persistence despite circumstance changes.

Anxiety disorders involve excessive worry, physical symptoms like racing heart or muscle tension, avoidance of feared situations, and significant distress. While everyone experiences anxiety occasionally, anxiety disorders involve symptoms that are disproportionate to actual threats, persist when no clear threat exists, and impair normal activities.

Changes in functioning signal possible mental health problems. Declining academic or work performance, withdrawing from social activities, neglecting self-care, or difficulty managing normal responsibilities all call for attention. Trust your feeling if someone seems significantly changed; reach out with concern.

Substance use becomes problematic when it interferes with responsibilities, relationships, or health, or when you use substances to cope with emotions or feel unable to function without them. Casual use differs from dependence, but the progression can be gradual.

If you or someone you know expresses thoughts of suicide or self-harm, take it seriously. These thoughts are symptoms of treatable conditions. Contact mental health professionals, crisis hotlines, or emergency services immediately. You cannot talk someone out of suicide, but you can connect them with proper help.

Reducing Stigma

Stigma surrounding mental health problems prevents many people from seeking help. This stigma is based on misunderstanding. Mental health conditions are no more shameful than diabetes or any other medical condition. They result from complex interactions of biology, psychology, and environment, not personal failure.

Language matters. Avoid describing people by their diagnoses: "person with depression" rather than "depressed person." Conditions are aspects of people's experience, not their entire identity.

Recognize that mental health difficulties affect people across all demographics. Mental health problems do not discriminate by intelligence, success, personality, or any other characteristic. No one is immune.

Seeking help is strength, not weakness. It shows self-awareness and willingness to address problems rather than allowing them to worsen. Many highly successful people manage mental health conditions with proper treatment.

Treatment Options

Effective treatments exist for virtually all mental health conditions. Treatment typically involves psychotherapy, medication, or combination of both, plus lifestyle modifications.

Psychotherapy involves structured conversation with trained professionals who help you understand patterns in thinking and behavior, develop coping strategies, process difficult experiences, and make beneficial changes. Different therapy approaches work better for different conditions and different people. Cognitive-behavioral therapy, interpersonal therapy, and dialectical behavior therapy have strong evidence for various conditions.

Medication can be highly effective for many mental health conditions. Antidepressants, anti-anxiety medications, mood stabilizers, and antipsychotic medications all have specific uses. Medication does not change your personality or make you a different person. It addresses biological dysfunctions that cause symptoms. Many people receive help from medication while also engaging in therapy.

Lifestyle factors significantly affect mental health. Regular exercise, adequate sleep, good nutrition, stress management, and social connection all support mental health. These are not substitutes for professional treatment when needed, but they are important components of comprehensive mental health care.

Treatment works but takes time. Improvement usually requires weeks or months, not days. Some treatments may not work for you specifically; finding the right approach sometimes requires trying several options. Persistence is important.

Seeking Help

Start by talking with your primary care provider. They can assess symptoms, rule out physical causes, provide initial treatment, and refer you to specialists if needed. Many people receive mental health treatment from primary care providers.

Mental health professionals include psychiatrists (medical doctors who can prescribe medication), psychologists (typically hold doctoral degrees and provide therapy), licensed clinical social workers, licensed professional counselors, and psychiatric nurse practitioners. All provide valuable services; the proper provider depends on your specific needs.

Many colleges and universities provide counseling services for students. These services are often free or low-cost and are designed to address common student mental health concerns.

Community mental health centers provide services regardless of ability to pay. If cost is a barrier, these centers can provide access to treatment.

Crisis resources are available 24/7. The National Suicide Prevention Lifeline (988) provides immediate support. Crisis text lines allow text-based communication. Hospital emergency departments can provide crisis assessment and referrals.

Be honest with providers about your symptoms and concerns. They cannot help effectively if they lack correct information. Everything you discuss is confidential except in specific legally defined circumstances involving danger to yourself or others.

Supporting Others

If someone you care about seems to be struggling with mental health, express concern directly but without judgment. "I've noticed you seem down lately and I'm worried about you" opens conversation without being accusatory.

Listen without trying to fix or minimize their experience. Sometimes people need to be heard more than they need advice. Avoid platitudes like "just think positive" or "it could be worse." These dismiss their experience.

Encourage professional help without insisting you have diagnosed them. "It sounds like you're really struggling. Have you thought about talking with a counselor?" is supportive without overstepping.

Offer practical help. Accompanying someone to appointments, helping with daily tasks, or just spending time together can all provide support.

Maintain boundaries. You can be supportive without taking responsibility for someone else's mental health. If supporting someone is significantly affecting your own wellbeing, seeking guidance about proper boundaries is important.

Take care of your own mental health. Supporting others who are struggling can be emotionally draining. Ensure you have support for yourself.

Building Mental Health Resilience

While you cannot prevent all mental health problems, you can build resilience that reduces risk and promotes faster recovery when problems do occur.

Maintain strong social connections. Relationships buffer against mental health difficulties and provide support when problems arise.

Develop healthy coping mechanisms before you need them. Having a repertoire of stress management techniques, enjoyable activities, and ways to process difficult emotions provides resources during challenging times.

Practice self-awareness. Recognizing early warning signs of declining mental health allows earlier intervention before problems become severe.

Address small problems before they become large ones. If you notice symptoms of depression or anxiety, implementing self-care strategies and seeking support early prevents escalation.

Remember that asking for help is normal and healthy. You would not hesitate to seek treatment for a broken bone. Mental health deserves the same attention and care as physical health.

The Road Ahead

Mental health is essential to overall wellbeing and deserves active attention. Mental health problems are common, treatable, and nothing to be ashamed of. Recognizing warning signs, seeking help when needed, and using effective treatments enables recovery and maintenance of good mental health.

Treatment works. Most people with mental health conditions improve significantly with proper care. The key is accessing that care rather than struggling alone with treatable conditions.

Prioritizing mental health through regular self-care, supporting strong relationships, developing healthy coping strategies, and seeking professional help when needed builds resilience and enables you to function effectively even during difficult periods. Your mental health affects every aspect of your life; investing in it provides enormous returns.

Chapter 18: Build Positive Relationships

Relationships profoundly affect wellbeing. Strong positive relationships provide emotional support, reduce stress, increase life satisfaction, and even improve physical health. Conversely, problematic relationships drain energy, increase stress, and undermine mental health. Understanding how to build and support healthy relationships while addressing or ending unhealthy ones is essential self-care.

The Importance of Positive Relationships

Research consistently shows that relationship quality predicts wellbeing more strongly than most other factors. People with strong social connections experience better mental health, greater life satisfaction, and longer lifespans than socially isolated people. The effect size is substantial, comparable to the impact of smoking on physical health.

Positive relationships provide emotional support during difficult times, practical help when needed, companionship that enriches daily life, and sense of belonging that counters isolation. They provide opportunities to be authentic, to be valued for who you are, and to contribute meaningfully to others' lives.

Quality matters more than quantity. A few close, supportive relationships provide more benefit than many superficial connections. You cannot support deep relationships with unlimited people. Focus energy on relationships that are mutually beneficial and genuinely enriching.

Characteristics of Healthy Relationships

Healthy relationships, whether friendships, romantic partnerships, or family connections, share common characteristics. Understanding these qualities helps you find which relationships to invest in and how to strengthen existing connections.

Mutual respect forms the foundation of healthy relationships. Both parties value each other's thoughts, feelings, needs, and boundaries. Disagreement does not require disrespect. You can have different views while still treating each other with consideration.

Trust develops through consistent reliability. You follow through on commitments. You support confidences. You are honest. Trust allows vulnerability, which deepens intimacy. Without trust, relationships are still superficial because neither person feels safe being authentic.

Communication is direct, honest, and respectful. You can express needs, concerns, and feelings without attacking the other person. You listen to understand their perspective rather than simply waiting to respond. Conflict is addressed rather than avoided or allowed to fester.

Reciprocity means both people invest in the relationship. Support, effort, and care flow in both directions. One-sided relationships where all giving comes from one person are unsustainable. Balance does not need exact equivalence at every moment, but overall patterns should be mutual.

Autonomy is preserved. Healthy relationships enhance both people's lives while allowing each person to keep independence, pursue individual interests, and keep other relationships. Healthy attachment does not require constant contact or abandonment of separate identity.

Growth is supported. People in healthy relationships encourage each other's development, celebrate successes, and provide support during challenges. They want each other to thrive, not to stay limited for the sake of the relationship.

Building New Relationships

Building relationships requires initiative and investment. Friendships do not typically develop without effort. You must spend time together, show interest in each other's lives, and show reliability.

Proximity matters significantly. You build relationships more easily with people you meet regularly through work, education, shared activities, or living situations. Shared circumstances offer natural opportunities for interaction and conversation topics.

Join groups aligned with your interests. Hobby groups, athletic teams, volunteer organizations, religious communities, professional associations, and similar contexts provide opportunities to meet people with shared interests. Shared activities help relationship development because you have concrete things to do together and discuss.

The Road Ahead

Positive relationships are essential to wellbeing. Strong connections provide emotional support, practical help, companionship, and sense of belonging. Building and keeping healthy relationships requires deliberate effort: showing genuine interest in others, being reliable, communicating directly, and investing time consistently.

Chapter 19: Practice Mindfulness

Mindfulness is the practice of paying attention to present moment experience with openness and without judgment. Despite sounding abstract, mindfulness is a concrete practice with measurable benefits for stress reduction, emotional regulation, focus, and overall wellbeing. Developing mindfulness skills requires practice but produces substantial returns.

Understanding Mindfulness

Mindfulness involves deliberately focusing attention on present moment experience: physical sensations, thoughts, emotions, and environmental stimuli. This contrasts with the typical mental state of dwelling on the past or worrying about the future while barely noticing what is actually happening now.

Benefits of Mindfulness

Research on mindfulness shows wide-ranging benefits. Regular practice reduces anxiety and depression, improves emotional regulation, enhances focus and cognitive function, reduces stress reactivity, and improves overall wellbeing.

Formal Mindfulness Practice

Formal practice involves setting aside dedicated time for structured mindfulness exercises. Start with brief sessions of five to ten minutes daily. Set a timer and sit comfortably with your spine straight, either in a chair with feet flat on the floor or cross-legged on a cushion.

Breath awareness is the most common starting point. Focus attention on the physical sensation of breathing. When your mind wanders, notice this without judgment and redirect attention to your breath. The wandering and redirecting is the practice.

Informal Mindfulness Practice

Informal practice involves bringing mindful awareness to routine activities. Choose one routine activity to do mindfully each day: brushing teeth, showering, eating, or walking. Instead of doing it on autopilot, pay attention to the actual experience: sensations, movements, sights, sounds, smells.

The Road Ahead

Mindfulness is the practice of deliberate attention to present moment experience with openness and acceptance. Research shows substantial benefits for mental health, emotional regulation, focus, stress management, and overall wellbeing. The benefits compound over time, producing effects that dramatically improve both immediate functioning and long-term health outcomes.

Chapter 20: Set Boundaries

Boundaries are limits you set up about what behaviors you will accept from others and what you will give of yourself. Clear boundaries protect your wellbeing, preserve your energy for what matters, and enable healthy relationships. Without boundaries, you become overwhelmed by others' demands and resentful of relationships that should be sources of support.

Understanding Boundaries

Boundaries define where you end and others begin. They set up what you are and are not responsible for, what treatment you will accept, and how you give your time and energy. Healthy boundaries are neither excessively rigid nor completely porous.

Why Boundaries Matter

Without clear boundaries, you become exhausted trying to meet everyone else's needs while neglecting your own. Resentment builds as you feel taken advantage of. Your actual capacity is finite. Refusing to acknowledge limits does not expand them; it guarantees overextension.

Identifying Your Boundaries

Many people have never explicitly considered their boundaries. They react to violations without having clearly defined what they will and will not accept. Finding boundaries begins with noticing what creates discomfort, resentment, or exhaustion.

Communicating Boundaries

Having boundaries means nothing if you do not communicate them. People cannot respect limits they do not know exist. Clear, direct communication of boundaries prevents most problems.

State boundaries explicitly rather than expecting others to intuit them. Use clear, direct language. You need not justify every boundary. Deliver boundary statements calmly and matter-of-factly.

Maintaining Boundaries

Stating boundaries is easier than keeping them. External pressure and internal guilt often lead people to relax boundaries they set up. Consistency is essential.

Follow through on boundaries. If you state a limit, keep it. Inconsistent enforcement teaches others that your boundaries are negotiable.

Respecting Others Boundaries

Healthy boundaries work both ways. Just as you have the right to show and keep limits, others have the same rights. Respecting others' boundaries shows the respect you want for your own.

When Boundaries Are Violated

Despite clear communication, boundaries will sometimes be violated. How you respond decides whether violations continue. Address violations directly and implement consequences for repeated violations.

Building Boundary Skills

Setting boundaries is a skill that improves with practice. If you have spent years without clear boundaries, implementing them feels uncomfortable initially. This discomfort decreases as boundary-setting becomes natural.

The Road Ahead

Boundaries protect your time, energy, physical space, emotional wellbeing, and right to make your own choices. Clear boundaries enable healthy relationships, prevent burnout, preserve authenticity, and allow sustainable self-care. Boundary-setting is a skill that develops with practice. The investment in developing boundary skills provides enormous returns in life quality.

Section 3: Financial Literacy

Financial literacy is essential for independent adult life. Money management affects your housing options, career choices, stress levels, and capacity to pursue goals. Poor financial skills create persistent problems: debt accumulation, inability to manage emergencies, and constrained life options. Good financial skills provide stability and expand possibilities.

Most high school curricula neglect practical financial education. You may understand complex mathematical concepts while lacking knowledge of budgeting, credit, taxes, or basic investing. This gap creates problems when you meet real financial decisions without adequate preparation.

This section addresses fundamental financial skills: understanding personal finance principles, creating and supporting budgets, managing debt, using credit responsibly, building savings and investments, and planning for major financial goals. These are not abstract concepts but practical tools you will use throughout your life.

Financial literacy develops through learning principles and applying them consistently. The strategies presented here are straightforward but require discipline to implement. Your financial success depends more on consistent application of basic principles than on sophisticated strategies or high income.

Chapter 21: Understanding Personal Finance

Personal finance encompasses all financial decisions individuals make: earning, spending, saving, investing, and protecting resources. Understanding these components and how they interact enables you to make informed decisions that support your goals rather than undermining them.

The Components of Personal Finance

Income is money you receive from employment, self-employment, investments, or other sources. Your income level matters, but how you manage available income matters more. Many high earners struggle financially due to poor management, while many moderate earners achieve financial security through sound practices.

Spending includes all money you pay for goods, services, and obligations. Some spending is fixed: rent, loan payments, insurance. Other spending is variable: food, entertainment, discretionary purchases. Understanding your spending patterns is essential for financial control.

Saving means setting aside money for future use rather than spending it immediately. Emergency funds, short-term goal savings, and long-term savings all serve different purposes. Adequate saving provides financial security and enables goal achievement.

Investing involves using money to buy assets expected to generate returns over time. This might include stocks, bonds, real estate, or business ownership. Investing builds wealth over the long term but involves risk and requires knowledge.

Protection involves insurance and other mechanisms that guard against financial catastrophe. Health insurance, auto insurance, renter's or homeowner's insurance, and eventually life and disability insurance all protect you from events that could destroy your finances.

Credit is the ability to borrow money with the promise to repay it. Used responsibly, credit enables purchases you could not otherwise make. Used irresponsibly, credit creates debt that constrains your financial freedom for years.

Financial Goals and Values

Effective personal finance begins with clarity about what you want money to enable. Without defined goals, financial decisions lack direction. You may earn adequate income while making poor choices because you have not found what you are trying to achieve.

Financial goals should be specific and concrete. "Be financially secure" is too vague to guide decisions. "Save $10,000 for emergencies," "Pay off student loans within five years," or "Save $50,000 for a home down payment" provide clear targets that inform spending and saving decisions.

Distinguish between short-term goals (achievable within a year), medium-term goals (one to five years), and long-term goals (beyond five years). Different time horizons require different strategies. Money needed next year should not be invested in volatile assets. Money needed in thirty years should not sit in low-interest savings accounts.

Your values should inform financial goals. If independence matters to you, prioritize ending debt and building emergency savings. If experiences matter more than possessions, distribute more to travel and activities. If family is central, factor in supporting relatives or saving for children's education. There is no universal correct allocation; align spending with what matters to you.

Recognize that goals will evolve as circumstances change. A goal structure proper at twenty-two differs from what makes sense at thirty or forty. Review and adjust goals periodically rather than assuming initial goals are still relevant indefinitely.

The Time Value of Money

Money available now is worth more than the same amount available later. This principle, called the time value of money, affects virtually all financial decisions. Understanding it helps you make better choices about saving, investing, and debt.

Money you have today can be invested to generate returns. One thousand dollars invested at a seven percent annual return becomes approximately $1,070 in one year, $1,967 in ten years, and $7,612 in thirty years. The same thousand dollars sitting uninvested is still worth one thousand dollars.

This principle makes early saving and investing powerful. Money invested in your twenties has decades to grow. Money invested in your fifties has less time to compound. A person who invests $5,000 annually from age twenty-two to thirty-two and then stops will accumulate more by retirement than someone who invests $5,000 annually from age thirty-two to sixty-two, assuming equivalent returns. Starting early matters enormously.

The time value of money also explains why debt is costly. When you borrow money, you pay interest. This means you ultimately pay more than the borrowed amount. A $10,000 loan at seven percent interest paid over five years costs approximately $11,900 total. That extra $1,900 is money you cannot save or invest. High-interest debt is particularly costly and should be eliminated quickly.

Inflation erodes money's purchasing power over time. Money sitting idle loses value as prices rise. This is another reason to invest rather than simply save in zero-interest accounts for long-term goals. Your investments must outpace inflation to support and grow real purchasing power.

Common Financial Mistakes

Understanding common errors helps you avoid them. Many financial problems stem from predictable mistakes rather than unusual circumstances.

Living beyond your means is the most fundamental error. If you consistently spend more than you earn, you accumulate debt. This is mathematically unsustainable. Eventually, you face crisis when you can no longer borrow or when debt payments consume too much income. The solution is straightforward but difficult: spend less than you earn, consistently.

Lacking emergency savings creates vulnerability. Unexpected expenses are inevitable: car repairs, medical bills, job loss. Without savings, you must borrow to manage these situations, often at high interest rates. This converts temporary problems into long-term financial damage. Building emergency savings should be an early financial priority.

Misusing credit card debt traps many people. Credit cards enable spending money you do not have. If you carry balances and pay only minimum payments, interest charges accumulate rapidly. A $5,000 credit card balance at eighteen percent interest, paying only minimums, takes over 25 years to eliminate and costs approximately $7,000 in interest. This transforms purchases you could not afford into purchases you truly cannot afford.

Not saving for retirement when young is a mistake with enormous long-term cost. The compounding returns from early retirement saving far exceed what you can achieve starting later, even if you eventually contribute more total dollars. If your employer offers retirement plan matching, not contributing enough to receive the full match is literally refusing free money.

Making major purchases impulsively rather than planning leads to poor decisions and often excessive debt. Large purchases—cars, furniture, electronics—should be deliberate decisions based on need and affordability, not impulse or social pressure. Waiting 24 to 48 hours before major purchases allows emotion to subside and rational evaluation.

Ignoring insurance needs creates catastrophic risk. An uninsured medical emergency, car accident, or apartment fire can destroy finances you spent years building. Adequate insurance is not optional; it is essential protection against low-probability, high-impact events.

Financial Planning Process

Systematic financial planning provides structure for making sound decisions. While your specific situation is unique, the general process applies broadly.

Assess your current situation honestly. Calculate your net worth: total assets minus total liabilities. Assets include savings, investments, and valuable possessions. Liabilities include all debts. Your net worth may be negative early in your career, particularly with student loans. This is not inherently problematic if you have a plan for improvement.

Track your income and spending for at least one month, preferably three. You cannot manage finances without knowing where money goes. Many people are shocked to discover their actual spending patterns. Tracking reveals discretionary spending that adds up substantially: frequent restaurant meals, subscriptions you barely use, impulse purchases. Awareness enables change.

Find your financial goals with specific targets and timeframes. Separate needs from wants. Needs are essentials: housing, food, healthcare, transportation to work. Wants are everything else. You can choose to prioritize some wants highly but distinguish them from needs.

Create a plan to achieve goals. This typically involves budgeting to ensure spending aligns with priorities, debt reduction if you carry high-interest debt, building emergency savings, and beginning to save for larger goals. The sequence matters: address highest-priority items before lower-priority ones.

Implement your plan consistently. Financial success is less about perfect planning than about adequate planning executed consistently. A simple plan you follow is superior to a best plan you abandon.

Review and adjust regularly. Circumstances change. Goals evolve. Strategies that worked at one point may need modification. Review your financial situation at least annually, more often during major life transitions.

Financial Information Sources

Financial literacy requires ongoing learning. The financial landscape changes: new products appear, regulations shift, investment options evolve. Staying informed helps you make better decisions.

Government resources provide free, unbiased financial information. The Consumer Financial Protection Bureau offers educational materials about credit, debt, banking, and consumer rights. The Federal Trade Commission provides guidance on avoiding scams and understanding credit reports. These are authoritative sources not trying to sell you products.

Nonprofit organizations focusing on financial literacy offer educational resources and sometimes counseling. The National Endowment for Financial Education, Jump$tart Coalition, and similar organizations provide quality educational materials.

Books by reputable financial experts offer comprehensive guidance. Look for authors with relevant credentials and histories. Be skeptical of get-rich-quick schemes or strategies promising exceptional returns with little risk. If something sounds too good to be true, it almost certainly is.

Financial professionals—certified financial planners, accountants, credit counselors—can offer personalized guidance for complex situations. Seek fee-only advisors who are compensated for advice rather than commissions on products they sell. This reduces conflicts of interest.

Be cautious about financial advice from unqualified sources. Friends, family, and internet strangers may mean well but lack expertise. Their situations differ from yours. What worked for them may not work for you. Verify advice against authoritative sources before acting on it.

The Road Ahead

Understanding personal finance principles is foundational to financial success. This includes recognizing the components of personal finance, aligning financial decisions with clear goals, understanding the time value of money, avoiding common mistakes, following a systematic planning process, and continuing to learn from reliable sources.

Financial literacy is not innate. It develops through education and practice. The fact that you were not taught these concepts in school does not mean you cannot learn them now. The investment in financial education provides returns throughout your life.

Your financial situation results primarily from decisions you make rather than circumstances you cannot control. While income level, family support, and economic conditions all matter, they matter less than your financial behaviors. Good decisions compound positively over time, as do poor decisions. The earlier you begin making sound financial decisions, the better your long-term outcomes.

Chapter 22: Budgeting Basics

A budget is a plan for your money. It specifies how you will distribute income to various categories: essential expenses, savings, debt payments, and discretionary spending. Budgeting prevents overspending, ensures important financial priorities are addressed, and provides clarity about your financial situation.

Many people resist budgeting, viewing it as restrictive or complicated. This perspective is counterproductive. A budget is not restriction but intentionality. Without a budget, you spend reactively based on immediate desires and end up unable to afford what truly matters to you. With a budget, you align spending with priorities and actually increase your financial freedom.

Why Budgeting Matters

Budgeting creates awareness. When you track income and expenses systematically, you understand your financial reality. Many people have vague notions about their finances that prove inaccurate when confronted with actual numbers. Spending adds up in ways you do not notice without tracking. Small daily purchases accumulate to substantial monthly expenses.

Budgets prevent overspending. When you distribute your income deliberately, you know what you can afford in each category. This prevents the common pattern of spending freely early in the month and scrambling to cover essentials later.

Budgeting ensures priorities are funded. Without explicit budgeting, important goals like emergency savings or debt repayment compete with immediate desires. You intend to save but never do because money disappears to discretionary spending. A budget distributes money to priorities first, treating them as non-negotiable rather than optional.

Budgets enable goal achievement. Financial goals require sustained effort over time. Budgeting creates the structure that converts intentions into actions. Each month you stick to your budget brings you closer to goals.

Budgeting reduces financial stress. Uncertainty about whether you can afford expenses creates anxiety. A budget provides clarity. You know what you can spend without jeopardizing other obligations. This knowledge reduces stress even when your budget is tight.

Creating Your Budget

Start by calculating your monthly income. Include all reliable income sources: salary or wages after taxes, regular freelance income, investment income, or other consistent sources. Use net income (after-tax amount) rather than gross income. If your income varies, use an average or estimate conservatively.

List all fixed expenses: costs that stay constant each month. This includes rent or mortgage, loan payments, insurance premiums, subscription services, and similar obligations. These are generally non-negotiable in the short term.

Estimate variable expenses: costs that fluctuate monthly. This includes groceries, utilities, transportation costs, personal care, and discretionary spending on entertainment, dining out, and hobbies. Review past spending to estimate realistic amounts. Do not underestimate; budgets based on wishful thinking fail.

Include irregular expenses that occur less than monthly but are predictable: annual insurance premiums, vehicle registration, holiday gifts, or seasonal costs. Calculate the annual total and divide by twelve to figure out the monthly amount you should set aside.

Allocate money to savings and financial goals. This should be treated as a fixed expense, not money left over after other spending. Common recommendations suggest saving at least ten to twenty percent of income, but any consistent saving is preferable to none. Prioritize emergency fund building if you lack adequate savings.

Compare total expenses to income. If expenses exceed income, you must reduce spending or increase income. This is mathematical reality. No budgeting technique enables sustainable spending above your income. Find areas to cut: reduce discretionary spending, cut subscriptions you barely use, cook more instead of eating out, or find cheaper alternatives for necessary expenses.

If income exceeds expenses, distribute the surplus purposefully. Direct it toward financial goals: building savings, increasing debt payments above minimums, or investing. Do not leave it as unallocated money that will disappear to impulse spending.

Budgeting Methods

Several budgeting approaches exist. Choose one that fits your situation and personality. The best budgeting method is one you will actually use consistently.

The 50/30/20 rule provides a simple framework. Allocate fifty percent of after-tax income to needs (housing, food, utilities, transportation, minimum debt payments), thirty percent to wants (entertainment, dining out, hobbies, nonessential purchases), and twenty percent to savings and debt payments beyond minimums. This is a starting framework, not a rigid rule. Your specific circumstances may require different allocations.

Zero-based budgeting assigns every dollar a specific purpose. Income minus all allocations equals zero. This ensures you deliberately decide how to use all available money rather than spending whatever stays after covering obvious expenses. Zero-based budgeting provides maximum control but requires more detailed tracking.

Envelope budgeting distributes cash to physical envelopes for different spending categories. When an envelope is empty, no more spending in that category until next month. This method provides tangible spending limits and prevents overspending. The modern digital equivalent involves using separate accounts or banking features that divide money into categories.

Pay yourself first prioritizes savings by automatically transferring money to savings accounts immediately when you receive income. You then budget remaining income for expenses. This ensures saving happens rather than depending on having money left over at month's end.

Tracking and Adjusting Your Budget

Creating a budget is insufficient. You must track actual spending against budgeted amounts and adjust as needed. Tracking reveals whether your budget is realistic and where overspending occurs.

Choose a tracking method you will use consistently. Options include spreadsheets, budgeting apps, pen and paper, or banking features that categorize spending. The specific tool matters less than consistent use. Review spending at least weekly to catch problems early.

When you overspend in a category, find why. Was your budget unrealistic? Did an unexpected expense occur? Was it impulse spending? Different causes require different responses. Unrealistic budgets need adjustment. Unexpected expenses highlight need for better irregular expense planning. Impulse spending requires better self-control and removing temptations.

Adjust your budget based on experience. Few people create perfect budgets initially. Over several months, patterns appear showing which categories need more or less allocation. Refine your budget to reflect reality while still working toward financial goals.

Expect imperfection. You will overspend some categories some months. This is normal. The goal is not perfect adherence but overall financial control. If you overspend one category, compensate by spending less in another. Review overall monthly spending rather than obsessing over individual categories.

Recalculate your budget when circumstances change significantly: income increases or decreases, you move, major expenses are eliminated or added, or financial goals change. A budget is a tool that should adapt to your situation, not a static plan you created once and never revisited.

Managing Irregular Income

Budgeting is more challenging with irregular income from freelancing, commission-based work, seasonal employment, or variable hours. However, budgeting is arguably more important in these situations because inconsistent income creates financial instability without careful management.

Calculate your average monthly income over the past six to twelve months. Use this as your baseline budget income. Some months you will earn more, others less. When you earn more than average, set aside the excess for months you earn less. This creates a buffer that smooths income fluctuations.

Prioritize building a larger emergency fund when you have irregular income. Three to six months of expenses is the standard recommendation, but six months or more provides better security with inconsistent income. This fund handles periods when income dips below expenses.

Budget essential expenses first. Ensure housing, utilities, food, insurance, and minimum debt payments are covered before distributing to discretionary spending. When income is lower than average, you may need to eliminate or severely reduce discretionary spending. When income is higher, resist the temptation to increase lifestyle spending; use extra income to build reserves.

Consider using percentage-based budgeting. Instead of fixed dollar amounts, distribute percentages of whatever you earn that month. Fifty percent for needs, thirty percent for wants, twenty percent for savings. This automatically scales spending to income level. You still need awareness to ensure spending in the 'needs' category covers essentials when income is low.

Reducing Expenses

When your budget shows expenses exceeding income, or when you want to accelerate financial goals, reducing expenses is necessary. Many people believe they have no room to cut spending. Detailed examination usually reveals options.

Start with discretionary spending. Entertainment, dining out, hobbies, and similar expenses are easiest to reduce without major lifestyle disruption. Cook at home rather than eating out. Choose free or low-cost entertainment. Postpone non-essential purchases. Small reductions across multiple categories add up substantially.

Examine subscriptions and memberships. Monthly subscription services are designed to be forgettable. Many people pay for streaming services they rarely use, gym memberships they do not use, or app subscriptions they forgot they had. Review all recurring charges and cut those not providing value proportional to their cost.

Reduce utility costs through conservation. Lower thermostats in winter, raise them in summer. Turn off lights and electronics when not in use. These changes are free and reduce monthly bills. The savings may seem small individually but compound over time.

Shop more strategically. Use lists to avoid impulse purchases. Compare prices across stores. Buy generic brands when quality is comparable. Use coupons and take advantage of sales for items you would buy anyway. Small savings per shopping trip accumulate to hundreds or thousands annually.

Consider larger changes for significant savings. Housing is typically the largest expense. If your rent or mortgage consumes too much of your income, moving to a less expensive place may be necessary. Transportation is another major expense. Could you use public transit instead of owning a car? Could you buy a reliable used car instead of a new one? These decisions have substantial financial impact.

Be strategic about what you cut. Some spending provides value beyond its cost: supporting physical health, keeping relationships, or supporting mental wellbeing. Dropping gym membership when you exercise regularly may save money short-term but cost more long-term in health problems. Cutting all social activities may damage relationships that provide important support. Make thoughtful trade-offs rather than cutting everything indiscriminately.

Increasing Income

While budgeting focuses primarily on managing expenses, increasing income is another approach to improving your financial situation. This is particularly valuable once you have reduced expenses to reasonable levels.

Seek raises or promotions in current employment. Document your contributions and accomplishments. Research market rates for your position. Ask for compensation that reflects your value. Many people never ask for raises and therefore never receive them.

Develop skills that increase your earning potential. More education, certifications, or technical skills can qualify you for better-paying positions. Consider whether the cost and time investment in skill development provides reasonable expected return in increased income.

Consider side income. Freelancing, part-time work, or monetizing skills or hobbies can supplement primary income. This is particularly possible early in your career before significant life responsibilities accumulate. Ensure added work does not compromise performance in your primary job or severely affect your health and relationships.

Sell items you no longer use. Most people accumulate possessions they do not need. Selling them generates one-time income while reducing clutter. This is not sustainable income but can provide short-term financial boost or help build emergency savings.

Common Budgeting Challenges

Understanding common obstacles helps you overcome them. Most budgeting failures stem from predictable problems.

Impulse spending undermines budgets. You create a reasonable plan but then make unplanned purchases that blow the budget. Combat this by implementing waiting periods for non-essential purchases, removing saved payment information from shopping sites, unsubscribing from marketing emails, and avoiding stores when you are bored or emotional. Impulse spending often stems from using shopping as entertainment or emotional coping rather than genuine need.

Social pressure complicates budgeting. Friends want to eat out, attend events, or make purchases that exceed your budget. This creates conflict between financial goals and relationships. Be honest about financial constraints. Suggest lower-cost alternatives. True friends will understand and accommodate. If people consistently pressure you to spend beyond your means, reconsider those relationships.

Unexpected expenses disrupt budgets. Cars break down. Medical issues arise. Appliances fail. While you cannot predict specific problems, you can predict that something will happen. This is why emergency funds are essential and why budgets should include irregular expense categories. When unexpected expenses occur, adjust spending in flexible categories to accommodate them rather than viewing your budget as failed.

Lifestyle inflation erodes financial progress. When income increases, spending increases proportionally or more. You upgrade housing, vehicles, wardrobes, and entertainment. This prevents the income increase from improving your financial position. When you receive raises or bonuses, keep existing spending levels and direct added income to savings, investments, or debt repayment. Some lifestyle improvement with increased income is reasonable, but automatic matching of spending to income prevents wealth accumulation.

Perfectionism causes budget abandonment. You overspend one category and declare the entire budget ruined. This all-or-nothing thinking is counterproductive. Budgeting is about overall patterns, not perfect execution. If you overspend, adjust and continue rather than giving up.

The Road Ahead

Budgeting is fundamental financial management. A budget provides awareness of your financial situation, prevents overspending, ensures priorities are funded, enables goal achievement, and reduces financial stress. Creating a budget involves calculating income, listing expenses, distributing money purposefully, and tracking actual spending against plans.

Multiple budgeting methods exist. The 50/30/20 rule, zero-based budgeting, envelope budgeting, and pay-yourself-first approaches all work when implemented consistently. Choose methods that fit your personality and circumstances. Adjust your budget as experience reveals what works for your situation.

Budgeting is not one-time activity but ongoing practice. You create initial budgets, track spending, adjust categories, respond to changing circumstances, and refine your approach over time. The discipline of consistent budgeting provides financial control that improves every aspect of your economic life. Starting now, regardless of current financial situation, it puts you on path to better financial outcomes.

Chapter 23: Managing Debt and Credit

Debt and credit are interconnected financial tools that require understanding and careful management. Used responsibly, they enable purchases and investments you could not otherwise make. Used poorly, they create financial stress that persists for years. Understanding how debt and credit work, their benefits and risks, and strategies for responsible use is essential financial literacy.

Understanding Debt

Debt is money you owe to lenders. You receive funds now in exchange for promising to repay them over time, typically with interest. The interest compensates lenders for risk and for forgoing other uses for their money.

Not all debt is equivalent. Distinction between productive debt and consumer debt matters. Productive debt finances assets that appreciate or generate income: student loans that increase earning potential, mortgages on property that builds equity, or business loans that create revenue. Consumer debt finances depreciating assets or consumables: credit card balances for restaurants and entertainment, auto loans for vehicles that lose value, or personal loans for vacations.

Types of Credit and Interest

Credit cards provide revolving credit with no fixed repayment term. You can borrow up to your credit limit, repay, and borrow again. If you carry balances, you pay interest, typically at high rates ranging from fifteen to twenty-five percent or more. Paying your full statement balance each month avoids interest charges entirely.

Personal loans provide fixed amounts repaid over fixed terms with set monthly payments. Interest rates vary based on creditworthiness and loan purpose, typically ranging from six to thirty-six percent. Payment amounts stay constant, making budgeting straightforward.

Student loans finance education. Federal student loans typically offer lower interest rates and more flexible repayment options than private loans. Interest rates and terms depend on loan type and when loans were originated. Understanding your specific loan terms is essential.

Auto loans finance vehicle purchases, typically secured by the vehicle. Because the loan is secured, interest rates are generally lower than unsecured personal loans or credit cards. Typical terms range from three to seven years, though longer terms exist. Longer terms mean lower monthly payments, but more total interest paid.

Mortgages finance home purchases, secured by the property. These are typically long-term loans with fifteen-to-thirty-year terms and relatively low interest rates compared to other debt. The total interest paid over a mortgage's life can exceed the loan principal due to long repayment periods.

The Cost of Debt

Interest significantly increases the cost of purchases made with debt. A $5,000 purchase financed on a credit card at eighteen percent interest, paying only minimum payments, takes approximately 25 years to repay and costs roughly $7,000 in interest. The actual cost is $12,000 for something priced at $5,000.

This shows why carrying credit card balances is extremely expensive. If you cannot afford something without debt, borrowing to buy it makes it even less affordable. The exception is when debt finances something that increases your income or reduces expenses by more than the interest cost.

Credit Scores

Your credit score is a numerical representation of your creditworthiness, typically ranging from 300 to 850. Lenders use credit scores to decide whether to extend credit and at what terms. Higher scores qualify you for better interest rates, which can save thousands of dollars over a loan's life.

Credit scores are calculated based on several factors. Payment history is most important, accounting for approximately 35 percent of your score. Making payments on time consistently builds good credit. Late payments, defaults, and bankruptcies severely damage scores. Credit use, the ratio of your credit card balances to limits, accounts for about 30 percent. Keeping use below thirty percent is ideal; below ten percent is better.

Length of credit history matters, accounting for fifteen percent. Older accounts help your score. This is why closing old credit cards can hurt your score even if you no longer use them. Credit mix, having different types of credit, accounts for ten percent. New credit inquiries account for ten percent; applying for many credit accounts in short periods hurts your score.

Building Good Credit

If you lack credit history, building it requires showing responsible borrowing. Start with a secured credit card, where you deposit money as collateral. Use the card for small purchases and pay the full balance monthly. This shows payment history without risk of accumulating debt.

Becoming an authorized user on a parent's or family member's credit card can help if they have good credit. Their payment history appears on your credit report, helping you build credit without primary responsibility for the account. Ensure the primary account holder keeps good payment history, as negative marks also affect authorized users.

Pay all bills on time. While utility and phone bills may not appear on credit reports when paid on time, late payments can be reported and damage credit. Consistent on-time payment across all obligations shows reliability.

Monitor your credit reports regularly. You are entitled to free annual credit reports from each of the three major credit bureaus. Review them for errors and dispute inaccuracies. Errors can significantly damage credit scores.

Managing Credit Card Debt

Credit card debt is particularly problematic due to high interest rates and psychological factors that encourage overspending. Managing it requires specific strategies.

Pay more than minimum payments. Minimum payments are calculated to maximize interest revenue for credit card companies, typically two to three percent of balances. Paying only minimums means debt persists for decades. Pay as much above minimums as possible to reduce principal and total interest paid.

Prioritize high-interest debt. If you have multiple credit cards, pay minimums on all but focus extra payments on the highest-interest card. After cutting that balance, redirect payments to the next highest rate. This debt avalanche method minimizes total interest paid.

Alternatively, the debt snowball method focuses on smallest balances first regardless of interest rates. This provides psychological wins as you drop accounts, building momentum. Financially, the avalanche method is superior, but the snowball method works better for some people psychologically.

Consider balance transfer cards for high-interest debt. Some cards offer zero percent interest for twelve to eighteen months on transferred balances. This allows you to make progress on principal without accumulating new interest. Ensure you can pay off the balance before the promotional period ends and read terms carefully, as balance transfers typically incur fees.

Using Credit Responsibly

Credit cards offer benefits when used responsibly: rewards programs, purchase protection, building credit history, convenience, and fraud protection. To gain these benefits without incurring debt, treat credit cards as payment tools rather than borrowing tools.

Pay statement balances in full every month. If you cannot afford a purchase without credit card debt, do not make the purchase. This single rule prevents most credit card problems. The grace period between purchase and payment due date provides free short-term credit. Using it without carrying balances provides convenience without cost.

Use credit cards for planned purchases you would make anyway, not to enable spending beyond your means. Allocate money in your budget for purchases, then use your credit card for those purchases. When the statement arrives, pay it from the money you have already given.

Set up automatic payments for at least the smallest amount due. This prevents late payments due to forgetfulness. Ideally, automate full balance payment if your budget consistently supports it.

Keep credit use low. Even if you pay balances in full, high use relative to limits can temporarily lower credit scores. If you are spending regularly approaches your limits, request credit limit increases or spread purchases across multiple cards.

Avoiding Common Credit Pitfalls

High-interest rates make credit card debt particularly expensive. People with excellent credit pay fifteen to twenty percent interest. Those with poor credit pay twenty-five percent or more. At these rates, balances grow rapidly if you do not pay aggressively. Understanding this cost should motivate aggressive debt elimination.

Overspending is psychologically easy with credit cards. Unlike cash transactions with immediate payment, credit card purchases do not feel like spending money. Studies show people spend more when using credit cards compared to cash. Combat this by treating credit card spending as seriously as cash spending, tracking all purchases, and reviewing statements carefully.

Late fees and penalties add to debt costs. A single missed payment can trigger a $40 late fee plus a penalty interest rate increase to twenty-nine percent or higher, applied to your entire balance. This dramatically increases debt costs. Automatic minimum payments prevent this problem.

Damaged credit scores result from late payments, defaults, or high credit use. Poor credit makes future borrowing more expensive through higher interest rates or denial of credit applications. Jobs needing security clearances or involving financial responsibility may screen credit reports. Damaged credit creates problems extending beyond borrowing costs.

Over-reliance on credit for living expenses shows spending above your means. Using credit cards to buy groceries or pay utilities because you lack cash means your expenses exceed your income. This is unsustainable. You must reduce spending, increase income, or both. Continuing to rely on credit to cover living expenses guarantees escalating debt.

Protecting Yourself from Fraud

Credit card fraud and identity theft can damage your finances and credit. Protection requires vigilance about personal information security.

Never share credit card numbers, PINs, or security codes except when making legitimate purchases with reputable merchants. Be skeptical of unsolicited calls or emails requesting financial information. Legitimate institutions do not request sensitive information via these channels.

Review credit card statements carefully each month. Find and dispute unauthorized charges immediately. Most credit card companies provide zero fraud liability for promptly reported fraudulent charges.

Monitor your credit reports regularly for accounts you did not open or inquiries you did not authorize. These show potential identity theft. Early detection allows faster resolution.

Use strong unique passwords for online banking and credit card accounts. Enable two-factor authentication when available. These precautions reduce unauthorized account access risk.

The Road Ahead

Debt and credit require careful management. Understanding different debt types, credit score mechanics, and responsible credit use enables you to use these tools' benefits while avoiding their pitfalls. Building good credit, managing debt strategically, using credit cards responsibly, and protecting against fraud all contribute to financial health. The habits you develop now about debt and credit affect your financial life for decades.

Chapter 24: Saving and Investing Basics

Introduction

A budget is the plan; saving and investing are the execution that builds security. This chapter focuses on what to do *after* your budget is in place: how to build an emergency fund, how to save for near-term goals without going into debt, and how to start investing for long-term goals like retirement.

Saving protects you from predictable shocks and unexpected emergencies. Investing grows your money over time so that inflation does not quietly reduce your purchasing power. Both need consistency more than complexity: regular contributions, a clear goal and timeline, and behavior that stays steady when markets or life get noisy.

You will learn how to set practical savings targets, choose proper places to keep your savings, begin investing with diversified, low-cost options, and use retirement accounts effectively. (Budgeting fundamentals are covered in Chapter 22, and debt/credit mechanics are covered in Chapter 23.)

Building Savings: Emergency Fund and Sinking Funds

Start with an emergency fund. This is money set aside specifically for unexpected events: job loss, car repairs, medical costs, urgent travel, or any expense that would otherwise force you into high-interest debt. If you are starting from zero, your first target is a small buffer (for example, one month of essential expenses). Then build toward three to six months of essential expenses.

Use sinking funds for predictable expenses. Not all "surprises" are surprises. Annual insurance premiums, gifts, vehicle maintenance, school costs, and holidays are expected. A sinking fund is a dedicated pool you contribute to monthly so that when the expense arrives, you pay cash instead of borrowing.

Set targets based on goals and timelines. Money needed in the next 0–3 years should generally stay in safe, liquid accounts (for example, a high-interest savings account). Money needed in 3–5 years can still lean conservative. Money needed 10+ years out (like retirement) can usually take on more market risk because you have time to recover from downturns.

Choose the right place to hold savings. Emergency funds and near-term goal money should be accessible and low-risk. A separate savings account (or separate sub-accounts) helps prevent accidental spending. The exact institution matters less than three properties: (1) low/no fees, (2) liquidity when you need it, and (3) a competitive interest rate.

Automate your saving. Set an automatic transfer the day after payday into your emergency fund or goal accounts. Automation removes willpower from the equation and makes "saving" a system rather than a monthly decision.

Use simple tools that support consistency: automatic transfers, separate accounts for different goals, and a quick monthly review of contributions and balances. The best system is the one you will keep using. Complexity is only helpful if it increases follow-through.

Avoiding Debt While You Save

Saving is much harder when high-interest debt is growing in the background. In general, build a small emergency buffer first (so the next surprise does not go on a credit card), then focus on cutting high-interest debt, while still capturing any employer retirement match if available.

A simple prioritization order for many people looks like this:

1. **Starter emergency fund** (a small buffer).
2. **Employer match** (if offered) up to the match amount.
3. **High-interest debt** elimination (details in Chapter 23).
4. **Full emergency fund** (3–6 months of essentials).
5. **Long-term investing** (retirement and other long-horizon goals).

If you are already carrying debt, use Chapter 23 for the mechanics and payoff strategies; the key here is to make sure your savings plan does not get repeatedly reset by preventable borrowing.

Consider balance transfer opportunities for high-interest credit card debt. Some credit cards offer zero percent interest for twelve to eighteen months on transferred balances. Transferring a high-interest balance to a zero percent card allows every payment to reduce principal directly. Read the terms carefully: balance transfers typically incur a fee of three to five percent, and the interest rate after the promotional period may be high. The strategy works only if you pay off the transferred balance before the promotional period ends.

Consistent, prompt payments protect your credit score and avoid late fees. Late payments trigger penalty fees of twenty-five to forty dollars and can increase your interest rate to a penalty rate of twenty-nine percent or higher. A single late payment can also lower your credit score, increasing the cost of future borrowing. Automate at least minimum payments on all debts to prevent missed payments due to oversight.

Basics of Investing: Compounding, Diversification, and Time Horizon

Investing is how you put money to work over long periods. The core engine is compounding: returns generate returns, so small, consistent contributions made early can outgrow larger contributions started later.

Diversification reduces risk by spreading money across many investments instead of betting on a single stock, sector, or idea. A diversified portfolio can still drop in value in the short run, but it is less vulnerable to any single failure.

Time horizon decides risk. If you will need the money soon, avoid volatility. If you will not need the money for decades (retirement), short-term market swings matter less and staying invested matters more than trying to time entry and exit.

Start simple. Broad, low-cost diversified funds and consistent contributions generally beat frequent trading and hype-driven bets. Fees matter: small annual fee differences compound over decades into large dollar differences.

Investing for the Future

Investing is the process of using money to buy assets that are expected to increase in value or generate income over time. While saving preserves money, investing grows it. The distinction matters because inflation erodes the purchasing power of money sitting idle. Cash saved in a standard account loses value in real terms over time. Money invested in diversified assets historically grows at rates that exceed inflation, building actual wealth.

The most powerful advantage available to young investors is time. Compound returns, where investment gains generate their own gains, produce exponential growth over long periods. One thousand dollars invested at an average annual return of seven percent becomes approximately seven thousand six hundred dollars after thirty years without any added contributions. The same investment over ten years produces only about two thousand dollars. The majority of the growth occurs in the later years as compounding accelerates. Starting early, even with small amounts, produces dramatically better outcomes than starting later with larger amounts.

Diversification is the practice of spreading investments across different asset types to reduce risk. Stocks offer higher potential returns but greater short-term volatility. Bonds provide more stable returns but lower long-term growth. Real estate, international markets, and other asset classes each carry different risk profiles. A diversified portfolio balances these characteristics so that poor performance in one area is offset by performance in others. The specific allocation proper for you depends on your time horizon, risk tolerance, and financial goals, but the principle of diversification applies universally.

Retirement accounts offer significant tax advantages that accelerate wealth building. Employer-sponsored 401(k) plans allow you to contribute pre-tax income, reducing your current tax burden while your investments grow tax-deferred. Many employers match employee contributions up to a specified percentage, which is essentially additional compensation that you lose by not taking part. If your employer offers matching contributions, contributing at least enough to receive the full match should be an immediate priority. It is a guaranteed, immediate return on your investment.

Individual Retirement Accounts offer added tax-advantaged investing options. Traditional IRAs offer tax deductions on contributions with taxes paid upon withdrawal in retirement. Roth IRAs accept after-tax contributions but allow tax-free withdrawals in retirement, including all investment gains. For young investors in relatively low tax brackets, Roth IRAs are often helpful because tax-free growth over decades of compounding produces substantial benefits.

Investment success depends more on consistent behavior than on selecting perfect investments. Contributing regularly regardless of market conditions, supporting your allocation strategy during market downturns, and avoiding emotional reactions to short-term volatility produce better outcomes than trying to time the market. Historically, investors who stay invested through market cycles significantly outperform those who try to buy at lows and sell at highs. The discipline to keep your strategy during uncomfortable periods is more valuable than any specific investment choice.

Educate yourself continuously about investing principles. Understand the fees associated with investment accounts and funds, as even small differences in annual fees compound into significant amounts over decades. Learn to distinguish between legitimate investment education and sales pitches for specific products. Be skeptical of any investment promising guaranteed high returns, as all legitimate investments involve some degree of risk proportional to their potential return.

The Road Ahead

Saving and investing work together. Saving gives you stability and prevents small problems from becoming expensive debt. Investing builds long-term wealth through compounding so that your future is not limited to what you can earn in a single year. Keep it simple: automate contributions, match the tool to the timeline (cash for near-term goals, diversified investing for long-term goals), and stay consistent through normal market and life volatility. Use Chapter 22 to keep your budget aligned with these priorities.

Chapter 25: Entrepreneurship

Introduction

Entrepreneurship is the process of creating, launching, and running a business. It involves finding opportunities, committing resources, managing risk, and building something that provides value to customers in exchange for revenue. Entrepreneurship is not limited to technology startups or venture-backed companies. It includes freelance services, local businesses, online stores, consulting practices, and any other venture where you create and deliver value independently.

Starting a business offers significant potential rewards: income not limited by a salary structure, autonomy over your work, the ability to build equity in something you own, and the satisfaction of creating something that did not previously exist. It also involves significant challenges: financial risk, uncertain income, long working hours, and the requirement to develop competence across multiple domains simultaneously. Understanding both the opportunity and the difficulty is essential for making informed decisions about whether and when to pursue entrepreneurship.

This chapter covers the fundamental steps involved in starting a business, the common challenges that new entrepreneurs face, and the practical considerations that figure out whether a venture succeeds or fails.

Developing a Business Plan

A business plan is a structured document that defines what your business does, who it serves, how it generates revenue, and how it will run. It serves two purposes: it forces you to think systematically about every aspect of your venture before committing resources, and it communicates your plan to potential investors, lenders, or partners who need to evaluate whether to support it.

The core elements of a business plan include a description of your product or service, an analysis of your target market, an assessment of the competitive landscape, a marketing and sales strategy, an operational plan, and financial projections. Each element requires research and honest analysis rather than optimistic assumptions.

Your product or service description should clearly articulate what you offer and why customers would choose it over existing alternatives. This requires understanding not just what you want to sell but what problem you solve for customers. Businesses succeed when they provide value that customers are willing to pay for, not simply because the founder is enthusiastic about the idea.

Market research figures out whether sufficient demand exists for your offering. Find your target customers: who they are, where they are, what they currently use to address the problem you solve, and how much they spend. Analyze your competition: who else serves this market, what they do well, what they do poorly, and how you differentiate from them. Market research prevents the costly mistake of building a product or service that nobody wants or that cannot compete effectively against established alternatives.

Financial projections estimate your startup costs, ongoing expenses, expected revenue, and timeline to profitability. Be conservative in revenue estimates and

DAVID WEBB

generous in expense estimates. Underestimating costs and overestimating revenue are among the most common reasons new businesses fail. Your projections should include a realistic assessment of how long you can run before the business becomes self-sustaining, and how you will fund operations during that period.

Legal Structure and Registration

Choosing a legal structure for your business has implications for taxation, personal liability, and administrative requirements. The primary options include sole proprietorship, partnership, limited liability company, and corporation. Each carries different trade-offs.

A sole proprietorship is the simplest structure. You and the business are legally the same entity. Setup requires minimal paperwork, and all income flows directly to your personal tax return. The significant disadvantage is unlimited personal liability: if the business incurs debts or legal judgments, your personal assets are at risk. This structure is proper for low-risk businesses with minimal liability exposure.

A limited liability company separates the business from your personal assets. If the business incurs debts or faces lawsuits, your personal savings, home, and other assets are generally protected. LLCs offer flexibility in management structure and tax treatment while providing meaningful liability protection. For most small businesses, an LLC provides the best balance of simplicity and protection.

Corporations are more complex structures right for businesses that plan to raise outside investment, issue stock, or run at significant scale. They involve more administrative requirements including formal governance, annual meetings, and separate tax filings. Most new entrepreneurs do not need corporate structure initially but may convert to one as the business grows.

Regardless of structure, register your business with proper government authorities. This typically involves registering your business name, obtaining an employer identification number for tax purposes, and securing any permits or licenses needed for your industry and location. Requirements vary by jurisdiction. Research the specific requirements for your business type and location and consult a lawyer or accountant if the requirements are unclear. Compliance failures can result in fines, forced closure, or personal liability that could otherwise have been avoided.

Securing Funding

Most businesses require capital to launch. Startup costs include inventory or equipment, marketing, legal and accounting fees, technology, workspace, and operating expenses for the period before revenue covers costs. Accurately estimating these costs and securing adequate funding before launch prevents the common failure mode of running out of money before the business becomes practical.

Self-funding, or bootstrapping, means using personal savings or income from other sources to finance the business. This approach keeps full ownership and control but limits the scale of your initial launch and puts personal finances at risk. If you bootstrap, set up a clear limit on how much personal capital you are willing to invest and keep an emergency fund separate from business funds.

Small business loans from banks or credit unions provide capital with repayment terms and interest rates. Approval typically requires a solid business plan, good personal credit, and sometimes collateral. The Small Business Administration guarantees certain loans, reducing lender risk and making approval more accessible for new businesses. Loan payments are a fixed obligation regardless of business performance, so borrow conservatively.

Outside investors, whether angel investors or venture capital firms, provide capital in exchange for equity in your business. This means you give up a percentage of ownership and often some degree of control. Investor funding is right for businesses with high growth potential that need significant capital to scale. Most small or local businesses are not suitable candidates for investor funding, and founders should understand the implications of giving up equity before pursuing this path.

Marketing and Customer Acquisition

A business without customers is an expensive hobby. Developing a marketing strategy that effectively reaches your target audience is essential from the outset. Your marketing plan should define who your customers are, where to reach them, what message will resonate with them, and how much you can afford to spend on acquisition.

Digital marketing offers cost-effective options for new businesses. A professional website shows credibility and serves as a central information point. Social media presence on platforms where your target customers are active provides direct communication channels. Search engine optimization helps potential customers find you when searching for the products or services you offer. Email marketing enables direct communication with people who have already expressed interest. Each channel requires consistent effort to produce results.

Word of mouth is still one of the most effective marketing channels, particularly for local and service businesses. Delivering exceptional value to early customers generates referrals that cost nothing and carry high credibility. Ask satisfied customers for reviews, testimonials, and referrals. A small number of enthusiastic customers who actively recommend your business can drive growth more effectively than a large advertising budget.

Track the effectiveness of your marketing efforts. Know how much you spend to get each customer and how much revenue each customer generates. This information enables you to invest more in channels that produce results and drop those that do not. Marketing without measurement is guessing. Data-informed decisions produce better outcomes and more efficient use of limited resources.

Common Challenges for New Entrepreneurs

Inexperience across business functions is the most common challenge for first-time entrepreneurs. Running a business requires competence in sales, marketing, finance, operations, customer service, and often legal compliance. Nobody starts with ability in all these areas. Acknowledge your knowledge gaps honestly and address them through education, mentorship, or hiring people with complementary skills.

Limited financial resources constrain what new businesses can do. Marketing budgets, inventory, staffing, and technology all require capital that most new ventures have in limited supply. Effective resource management, focusing spending on the highest-impact activities and minimizing overhead, is critical during early stages when revenue has not yet reached sustainable levels.

Time management becomes challenging when you manage every aspect of operations. Without the structure of an employer-defined schedule, work can expand to fill every available hour. Establish clear working hours, prioritize tasks based on their impact on revenue and growth, and recognize that not every task deserves your personal attention. Learning to delegate, outsource, or defer low-priority work is essential for supporting both productivity and personal wellbeing.

Market competition means you rarely work without alternatives available to customers. Differentiating your business, whether through quality, service, specialization, pricing, or customer experience, decides whether customers choose you over competitors. Understand what your competitors offer and find specific areas where you can provide superior value. Competing on price alone is rarely sustainable for small businesses and often leads to insufficient margins to survive.

Mentorship significantly improves outcomes for new entrepreneurs. Experienced business operators can find problems you have not yet recognized, suggest solutions you would not discover independently, and provide perspective during difficult periods. Seek mentors through local business associations, industry groups, entrepreneurship programs, or direct outreach to business owners you respect. Most experienced entrepreneurs are willing to share knowledge with people who show genuine commitment and ask specific, thoughtful questions.

The Road Ahead

Entrepreneurship is a demanding but potentially rewarding path. Success requires thorough planning, adequate funding, effective execution, and the resilience to persist through inevitable setbacks. It is not a shortcut to wealth or an escape from the demands of employment. It is a different set of demands that offers different rewards.

Start with a solid business plan grounded in market research rather than assumptions. Secure adequate funding before launching. Follow legal requirements from the outset. Build marketing systems that consistently bring in customers. Manage your finances conservatively, particularly in the early stages when revenue is uncertain. Seek mentorship and be honest about what you do not know. Grow gradually, building a solid foundation before trying to scale.

Whether entrepreneurship becomes your primary career or an experience that develops skills you apply elsewhere, the planning, problem-solving, financial management, and persistence it requires are valuable in any professional context. Approach it with realistic expectations, thorough preparation, and commitment to continuous learning.

Section 4: Digital Skills

Digital competence is no longer optional. Nearly every professional field, personal financial transaction, and communication channel now runs through digital platforms. The ability to navigate these systems effectively decides your access to opportunities, your vulnerability to exploitation, and your capacity to take part meaningfully in modern economic and social life.

Despite the prevalence of technology, many people use digital tools without understanding how they function, what risks they present, or how to use them effectively. Familiarity with smartphones and social media does not constitute digital literacy. Knowing how to scroll through content is fundamentally different from understanding how to evaluate information sources, protect personal data, create digital products, or present yourself professionally online.

This section addresses four critical areas of digital competence. Digital literacy and online safety covers the foundational skills needed to navigate the internet critically and securely, including evaluating information, recognizing threats, and supporting proper digital conduct. Coding and programming basics introduces the logic and languages that underlie every digital tool you use, providing a foundation whether you pursue programming professionally or simply want to understand how software works. Social media management examines how to use platforms strategically rather than passively, whether for personal branding, professional purposes, or business goals. Cybersecurity and privacy addresses the specific threats to your personal information and the practices needed to protect yourself in an environment where data breaches, identity theft, and surveillance are persistent realities. Finally, online job search strategies covers the practical skills needed to navigate digital employment platforms, build a professional online presence, and conduct an effective job search.

The goal is practical competence. Each chapter provides specific knowledge and actionable practices rather than general awareness. Technology evolves rapidly, but the principles of critical evaluation, security consciousness, strategic communication, and systematic problem-solving remain constant regardless of which platforms or tools appear next.

Chapter 26: Digital Literacy and Online Safety

Introduction

Digital literacy extends far beyond the ability to use devices and applications. It encompasses the capacity to find, evaluate, create, and communicate information using digital technologies. It includes understanding how digital systems work, recognizing their limitations and risks, and using them responsibly. In an environment where misinformation spreads faster than verified reporting, where personal data has become a commodity, and where online interactions carry real-world consequences, digital literacy is a fundamental requirement for informed participation in society.

Most formal education provides minimal instruction in these areas. Students learn to use specific software applications but rarely develop the critical evaluation skills needed to assess the reliability of online information, the security awareness needed to protect personal data, or the ethical framework needed to conduct themselves responsibly in digital spaces. This chapter addresses these gaps directly, covering information evaluation, online safety practices, digital conduct, and the ongoing learning needed to remain competent as technology evolves.

Evaluating Information and Identifying Misinformation

The volume of information available online is unprecedented, and so is the volume of misinformation.

Anyone can publish content, and algorithmic distribution systems prioritize engagement over accuracy. Content that provokes strong emotional reactions spreads faster than balanced, factual reporting. This environment makes critical evaluation essential rather than optional.

Effective information evaluation begins with source assessment. Consider who created the content and what their qualifications, motivations, and potential biases are. Established news organizations, peer-reviewed journals, government statistical agencies, and recognized subject matter experts are generally more dependable than anonymous social media accounts, partisan blogs, or sites with unclear ownership. This does not mean established sources are infallible, but they typically work under editorial standards, correction policies, and reputational accountability that informal sources lack.

Examine the evidence supporting claims. Reliable information typically cites specific sources, references verifiable data, and distinguishes between established facts and interpretation. Be skeptical of content that relies on vague attributions, anonymous sources without corroboration, or emotional appeals without substantive evidence. Headlines designed to provoke outrage or disbelief are often misleading even when the underlying article has more nuance.

Cross-reference significant claims across multiple independent sources. If a story appears on only one site or only within a particular ideological ecosystem, treat it with added skepticism. Misinformation often circulates within closed networks where confirmation bias prevents critical examination. Checking whether reputable sources across the political spectrum are reporting the same basic facts provides a practical reliability test.

Understand the distinction between different types of problematic content. Misinformation is false or inaccurate content shared without malicious intent, often by people who believe it is true. Disinformation is deliberately fabricated or manipulated content created to deceive. Misinformation is genuine information shared out of context or selectively to mislead. Each needs different evaluation approaches, but all can cause harm when accepted uncritically.

Develop the habit of pausing before sharing content, particularly content that produces a strong emotional reaction. The impulse to immediately share something shocking, outrageous, or perfectly aligned with existing beliefs is precisely what misinformation exploits. Taking even a few minutes to verify claims before amplifying them reduces the spread of false information and protects your own credibility.

Online Safety and Personal Security

Online safety requires both technical measures and behavioral awareness. Technical measures include password management, authentication practices, software maintenance, and privacy configuration. Behavioral awareness involves recognizing social engineering attempts, understanding what information exposure means, and making informed decisions about digital interactions.

Password security is still the most fundamental protective measure. Use unique passwords for every account. Password reuse means that a single breach compromises all accounts sharing that password. Use a password manager to generate and store complex, unique passwords for each service. This ends the need to remember dozens of passwords while keeping strong security across all accounts.

Enable two-factor authentication on every account that supports it, particularly email, financial services, and social media. Two-factor authentication requires a second verification step beyond your password, typically a code sent to your phone or generated by an authenticator application. This means that even if someone obtains your password, they cannot access your account without the second factor. Authenticator applications are more secure than SMS-based codes, which can be intercepted through SIM-swapping attacks.

Keep all software updated. Security updates patch known vulnerabilities that attackers actively exploit. Delaying updates leaves your devices exposed to threats that have already been found and for which fixes exist. Enable automatic updates where possible and install updates promptly when notified.

Recognize phishing attempts. Phishing is the practice of sending fraudulent communications that appear to come from legitimate sources in order to obtain sensitive information. These messages often create urgency, claiming your account has been compromised, a payment has failed, or action is needed immediately. Legitimate organizations rarely request sensitive information via email or text message. When in doubt, contact the organization directly through their official website or phone number rather than clicking links in the message.

Be cautious about the information you share publicly. Social media profiles, public records, and data broker sites collectively provide substantial personal information that can be used for identity theft, social engineering, or targeted harassment. Review privacy settings on all platforms regularly. Limit the personal details visible to the public, including your full date of birth, home address, phone number, and current location.

Digital Conduct and Responsibility

Digital interactions carry real consequences. Content posted online is effectively permanent. Even removed posts may have been screenshotted, cached, or archived. Comments made in anger, photos shared impulsively, and opinions expressed without full consideration become part of your digital record, accessible to future employers, educational institutions, colleagues, and personal contacts.

Professional digital conduct follows the same principles as professional in-person conduct: communicate respectfully, consider your audience, and recognize that your behavior reflects on you. The perceived anonymity or distance of online communication does not end the impact of your words on others or the consequences for your own reputation.

Cyberbullying and online harassment cause measurable harm. If you see it, reporting and supporting targets is right. If you experience it, document the behavior through screenshots, use platform reporting tools, block offending accounts, and seek support from trusted individuals or authorities when necessary. Disengaging from hostile interactions is not weakness but a practical response that denies aggressors the reaction they look for.

Digital etiquette encompasses practical considerations that affect how others perceive you. In professional communications, use proper grammar and proper tone. In group discussions, stay on topic and respect others' perspectives. In shared digital spaces, follow established norms and guidelines. These practices seem minor individually but collectively decide whether others view you as someone they want to work with, collaborate with, or recommend.

Staying Current with Technology

Technology changes continuously. New platforms appear, existing services change their terms and features, and new threats develop alongside new capabilities. Supporting digital literacy requires ongoing attention rather than one-time learning.

Follow reputable technology news sources to stay informed about significant developments, particularly those affecting security and privacy. When new platforms or services become relevant to your professional or personal life, invest time in understanding their functionality, terms of service, and privacy implications before committing personal information or content.

Approach new technologies with balanced assessment rather than either uncritical enthusiasm or reflexive resistance. Evaluate what specific benefits a new tool provides, what information or access it requires, and whether the trade-off is worthwhile for your circumstances. Not every new platform or service merits adoption but dismissing technological developments without evaluation leaves you increasingly disconnected from the tools and systems that others use to communicate, work, and organize.

Digital literacy is not a fixed skill set but a continuous practice. The specific platforms and tools will change throughout your life, but the underlying competencies of critical evaluation, security awareness, responsible conduct, and adaptive learning remain relevant regardless of what technologies appear. Developing these competencies now shows patterns that serve you across every technological transition you meet.

Chapter 27: Coding and Programming Basics

Introduction

Programming is the process of writing instructions that computers execute. Every application on your phone, every website you visit, every algorithm that decides what content appears in your feed, and every automated system processing your financial transactions runs on code written by human beings. Understanding programming fundamentals provides insight into how these systems work, enables you to create digital tools yourself, and develops problem-solving capabilities that transfer to virtually every professional domain.

You do not need to become a professional software developer for programming knowledge to be valuable. Professionals across fields including finance, marketing, science, healthcare, and education increasingly benefit from the ability to automate repetitive tasks, analyze data, build simple tools, and communicate effectively with technical teams. Programming literacy is becoming analogous to statistical literacy: not everyone needs ability, but basic competence provides significant advantages.

This chapter introduces the foundational concepts of programming, surveys common languages and their applications, and offers practical guidance for beginning to learn. The goal is not mastery but sufficient understanding to figure out whether and how programming fits into your goals, and a clear starting path if you choose to pursue it.

Computational Thinking and Programming Logic

Before writing code, understanding the logical framework underlying programming is essential. Programming is fundamentally about decomposing problems into precise, sequential instructions that a computer can execute. Computers do exactly what they are told, nothing more. They do not infer intent or fill in gaps. This requires a level of precision in thinking that is valuable far beyond programming itself.

The core concepts of programming logic appear in every language and every application. Variables are named storage locations that hold data. They function as labeled containers: you assign a value to a variable name, and you can retrieve, change, or use that value later in your program. Variables can hold different types of data including numbers, text, lists, and more complex structures.

Conditionals allow programs to make decisions. An if-then-else structure evaluates whether a condition is true and executes different instructions depending on the result. This is how software responds to different inputs and situations. When you enter a password and the system either grants or denies access, a conditional is at work. When a website displays different content based on your location, conditionals decide what you see.

Loops enable programs to repeat operations. Rather than writing the same instruction a thousand times, a loop executes a block of code repeatedly until a specified condition is met. Processing every item in a list, checking each row of a spreadsheet, or refreshing a display at regular intervals all use loops. Understanding loops is understanding how computers manage scale, performing millions of repetitive operations that would be impractical for humans.

Functions are reusable blocks of code that perform specific tasks. Instead of rewriting the same sequence of instructions every time you need it, you define a function once and call it whenever needed. Functions make programs more organized, more readable, and easier to support. They also enable collaboration, as different people can write different functions that work together in a larger system.

These four concepts, variables, conditionals, loops, and functions, form the foundation of all programming. Regardless of which language you learn or what you build, you will use these constructs constantly. Mastering them provides a transferable foundation that makes learning any specific language substantially easier.

Programming Languages and Their Applications

Programming languages are the specific syntaxes used to write instructions for computers. Each language has its own rules, strengths, and typical use cases.

Choosing a first language depends on what you want to build and what learning experience you prefer.

Python is widely recommended as a first language due to its readable syntax and broad applicability. Python code resembles English more than most programming languages, making it accessible to beginners. It is used extensively in data analysis, artificial intelligence, web development, scientific computing, and automation. The language has a large community and extensive libraries, collections of pre-written code that provide functionality you can use without building from scratch. If you are uncertain where to start, Python is a strong default choice.

JavaScript is the language of the web. Every modern web browser executes JavaScript, making it the primary language for creating interactive websites and web applications. If you are interested in building websites, web-based tools, or front-end interfaces, JavaScript is essential. It also extends to server-side development, mobile applications, and desktop applications through various frameworks, making it one of the most versatile languages available.

Java is a general-purpose language known for its reliability and portability. It powers Android mobile applications, enterprise-level business systems, and large-scale backend infrastructure. Java enforces more structure than Python, which some learners find helpful for developing disciplined programming habits. Its verbose syntax means more typing but also more explicit, self-documenting code.

C++ provides low-level control over system resources and is used in performance-critical applications including game engines, operating systems, embedded systems, and high-frequency trading platforms. It is more complex than the languages above and has a steeper learning curve, but it provides deep understanding of how computers actually process instructions. Learning C++ is not necessary for most beginners, but it offers advantages for those interested in systems programming or performance-intensive applications.

The specific language matters less than the foundational understanding you develop. Learning one language well makes learning more languages significantly easier because the underlying concepts transfer. Syntax differs, but variables, conditionals, loops, and functions exist in every language. Choose based on your immediate goals and start building. You can always learn more languages as your needs evolve.

Learning to Program Effectively

Effective programming education combines conceptual understanding with practical application. Reading about programming without writing code is ineffective, as is writing code without understanding the principles behind it. Both theory and practice are necessary.

Begin with small, concrete projects. A calculator, a to-do list application, a simple webpage, or a script that automates a repetitive task provides immediate feedback and tangible results. Small projects teach fundamental concepts in context and produce something you can see working. This is more effective than abstract exercises disconnected from practical outcomes.

Expect errors. Programming involves continuous debugging, the process of finding and correcting mistakes in your code. Error messages are informational tools, not indicators of failure. They tell you precisely what went wrong and where. Learning to read error messages, find the cause, and implement corrections is a core programming skill, not a sign that something has gone wrong with your learning process.

Use available resources extensively. Online documentation, tutorials, forums, and community question-and-answer sites have solutions to virtually every common problem a beginner meets. Professional programmers routinely consult documentation and search for solutions to specific problems. This is standard practice, not a shortcut. The ability to find and apply relevant information efficiently is itself a valuable programming skill.

Consistency produces better results than intensity. Regular practice of thirty to sixty minutes daily builds skills more effectively than occasional marathon sessions. Programming requires building mental models that develop through repeated exposure and practice. Short, consistent sessions allow these models to combine between practice periods.

Engage with programming communities. Online forums, local meetup groups, open-source projects, and coding communities provide support, feedback, and exposure to how experienced programmers approach problems. Seeing different solutions to the same problem broadens your understanding and introduces techniques you would not discover independently.

Practical Applications Beyond Professional Development

Programming knowledge provides practical benefits even if you never work as a developer. Automating repetitive tasks, whether organizing files, processing data, or generating reports, saves significant time over a career. Understanding how software works enables you to use existing tools more effectively and communicate your needs more precisely when collaborating with technical teams.

Data analysis capabilities are increasingly valuable across professions. Basic programming enables you to process, analyze, and visualize data sets that would be impractical to manage manually. Marketing professionals analyze campaign performance, healthcare workers find patient trends, educators evaluate student outcomes, and business operators analyze financial metrics, all more effectively with basic programming skills.

Understanding programming also provides critical perspective on the automated systems that increasingly affect daily life. Algorithms decide what news you see, what products are recommended to you, how your credit application is evaluated, and whether your resume passes initial screening. Understanding the basic logic of these systems enables you to interact with them more effectively and evaluate their outputs more critically.

Whether programming becomes central to your career or stays a supplementary skill, the analytical thinking, systematic problem-solving, and comfort with technology that programming develops are assets in any field. The investment in learning fundamentals pays returns that extend well beyond the specific code you write.

Chapter 28: Social Media Management

Introduction

Social media platforms are communication tools. Like any tool, their value depends on how they are used. Passive consumption differs fundamentally from strategic use, and the difference has measurable consequences for professional opportunities, business outcomes, and personal brand development. Understanding how to manage social media effectively means moving from being a consumer of content to being a purposeful participant who uses these platforms to achieve specific goals.

Social media management encompasses strategy development, content creation, community engagement, analytics interpretation, and ongoing optimization. These skills apply whether you are building a personal professional presence, managing accounts for an employer, marketing a business, or promoting a creative endeavor. The principles of effective social media management remain consistent across platforms even as specific features and algorithms change.

This chapter covers the strategic foundations of effective social media use: defining goals, understanding audiences, creating engaging content, measuring results, and adjusting based on data. The goal is to move from reactive, unplanned social media use to intentional, strategic communication that serves your broader goals.

Developing a Social Media Strategy

Effective social media use begins with clearly defined goals. Without specific goals, social media activity becomes unfocused, and its impact becomes impossible to measure. Decide what you want to do: building professional visibility, driving traffic to a website, generating sales leads, setting up ability in a subject area, growing an audience for creative work, or something else entirely. Your goals decide which platforms to prioritize, what content to create, and how to evaluate success.

Understanding your target audience is equally essential. Effective communication requires knowing who you are trying to reach, what they value, where they spend their time online, and what type of content they engage with. A message that resonates with business professionals on LinkedIn requires different formatting, tone, and content than one targeting creative communities on Instagram or technical audiences on specialized forums. Research your audience through platform analytics, competitor analysis, and direct engagement.

Consistency in posting schedule and content quality builds audience trust and algorithmic favourability. Most platform algorithms reward accounts that post regularly and generate consistent engagement. Develop a content calendar that plans posts in advance, ensuring regular output without the stress of daily improvisation. Planning ahead also enables more thoughtful content creation and better alignment between individual posts and your overall strategy.

Platform choice should be strategic rather than reflexive. You do not need to keep an active presence on every platform. Find where your target audience is most active and where your content format is most effective, then concentrate your effort there. A strong presence on two platforms produces better results than a weak presence on six.

Creating Content That Generates Engagement

Content quality decides whether your audience grows, engages, and takes desired actions. Quality in the social media context means content that provides value to your audience, whether through information, entertainment, inspiration, or utility. Content that serves only self-promotion without offering value to the viewer generates minimal engagement and often drives audience loss.

Visual quality matters significantly on visually oriented platforms. Clear images, consistent visual branding, and professional presentation signal credibility. This does not require expensive equipment or professional design skills. Consistent color schemes, clean compositions, and readable text overlays are achievable with basic tools and attention to detail.

Written content should communicate clearly and concisely. Captions and text posts should convey their message efficiently while supporting your authentic voice. Ask questions to invite responses. Share specific insights rather than generic statements. Tell stories that illustrate points concretely rather than saying abstract principles. Content that prompts interaction, whether through questions, calls to action, or thought-provoking perspectives, generates more engagement than passive broadcasts.

Hashtags and keywords function as discovery mechanisms on most platforms. Research which tags are relevant to your content and audience. Use specific, targeted hashtags rather than only broad, high-competition ones. A post tagged with a niche-specific term reaches a more relevant audience than one tagged only with generic terms that attract millions of unrelated posts.

Engagement is reciprocal. Responding to comments, taking part in discussions on others' content, and building relationships with other creators and community members generates more sustainable growth than broadcasting content without interaction. Social media platforms are designed for conversation. Accounts that take part in dialogue rather than monologue consistently outperform those that only broadcast.

Analytics and Optimization

Social media platforms provide analytics tools that show how your content performs. These metrics enable evidence-based decision-making rather than guesswork about what works. Key metrics include reach, which measures how many unique users saw your content; engagement rate, which measures the percentage of viewers who interacted with your content; click-through rate, which measures how many viewers took a desired action; and follower growth, which indicates whether your audience is expanding.

Analyze which content types, topics, posting times, and formats generate the strongest results. Patterns in your analytics reveal what your audience values and when they are most receptive. Use this information to adjust your strategy, producing more of what works and less of what does not. This iterative process of creating, measuring, and adjusting is fundamental to effective social media management.

Set realistic benchmarks based on your current performance rather than comparing yourself to accounts with vastly different audiences, resources, or histories. Meaningful growth metrics track improvement over your own baseline: increasing engagement rates, growing reach, improving click-through rates, and expanding your audience steadily over time.

Experimentation is essential. Assess different approaches systematically: try different content formats, posting frequencies, caption styles, and engagement strategies. Track results for each variation. What works for one audience on one platform may not work for another. Your analytics provide the feedback needed to refine your approach continuously based on evidence rather than assumption.

Managing Your Professional Online Presence

Your social media profiles function as a public portfolio. Potential employers, clients, collaborators, and professional contacts will search for you online, and what they find shapes their impression before any direct interaction occurs. Managing your online presence deliberately ensures that this impression supports rather than undermines your professional goals.

Audit your existing social media profiles from the perspective of someone who knows nothing about you. Review all public content, photos, comments, and associated accounts. Remove or restrict content that conflicts with the professional image you want to project. This is not about being inauthentic but about exercising proper judgment about what you present publicly, the same judgment you apply when choosing what to wear to a professional meeting.

Separate personal and professional content were proper. Many people keep distinct accounts for personal and professional use. This allows you to support privacy in your personal life while presenting a curated professional image. If you use a single account for both purposes, configure privacy settings carefully and consider your audience before every post.

Protect your mental health in relation to social media use. Monitor how time spent on platforms affects your mood, self-perception, and productivity. Set boundaries around usage, including specific times for checking platforms and specific durations for browsing. Unfollow or mute accounts that consistently produce negative emotional responses. Social media should be a tool that serves your goals, not a compulsion that undermines your wellbeing.

Chapter 29: Cybersecurity and Privacy

Introduction

Cybersecurity and privacy are practical necessities in a world where personal, financial, and professional information exists primarily in digital form. Data breaches expose millions of records annually. Identity theft affects a significant percentage of adults each year. Ransomware attacks disable businesses, hospitals, and government systems. These are not theoretical risks but routine events that affect ordinary individuals.

Cybersecurity refers to the practices and technologies that protect digital systems, networks, and data from unauthorized access, damage, or theft. Privacy concerns what personal information exists about you, who has access to it, and how it is used. Both require active management. Default settings on most devices and platforms prioritize convenience over security and data collection over privacy. Protecting yourself requires deliberate configuration and consistent habits.

This chapter covers the primary threats to your digital security and privacy, the protective measures available to you, and the habits needed to keep protection over time. The goal is not to make you a cybersecurity expert but to equip you with the practical knowledge needed to protect your personal information, financial accounts, and digital identity from the most common threats.

Understanding Common Threats

Phishing is still the most prevalent cyberattack method. Phishing attacks use fraudulent emails, text messages, or websites that impersonate legitimate organizations to trick you into revealing sensitive information such as passwords, credit card numbers, or social security numbers. These messages have become increasingly sophisticated, often replicating the exact visual design and language of legitimate communications from banks, employers, government agencies, and technology companies.

Finding phishing attempts requires attention to specific indicators. Check the sender's actual email address, not just the display name, as phishing emails often use addresses that closely resemble but do not match legitimate domains. Look for urgency language designed to prevent careful consideration, such as threats of account closure or claims of unauthorized activity requiring immediate action. Hover over links before clicking to verify that the actual URL matches the claimed destination. When uncertain, navigate to the organization's website directly rather than following links in the message.

Malware encompasses various forms of malicious software designed to compromise your devices. Viruses attach to legitimate programs and spread when those programs execute. Trojans disguise themselves as useful software to gain access to your system. Spyware watches your activity and collects information without your knowledge. Ransomware encrypts your files and demands payment for the decryption key. Malware typically enters systems through email attachments, compromised websites, infected downloads, or removable storage devices.

Social engineering attacks exploit human psychology rather than technical vulnerabilities. Attackers manipulate people into revealing information or taking actions that compromise security. This includes pretexting, where attackers create fabricated scenarios to justify requesting information, and baiting, where attackers leave infected devices or files where targets will find them. Social engineering succeeds because it targets trust, helpfulness, fear, and urgency, emotions that override careful judgment.

Man-in-the-middle attacks intercept communications between two parties, allowing attackers to read, change, or redirect information in transit. These attacks are particularly common on unsecured public Wi-Fi networks, where attackers can position themselves between your device and the network to capture data you send, including login credentials and financial information.

Protective Measures

Password management is the foundation of personal cybersecurity. Use a password manager to generate and store unique, complex passwords for every account. Your passwords should be long, at least twelve characters, and have a mix of uppercase and lowercase letters, numbers, and symbols. Never reuse passwords across multiple accounts. A single breach that exposes a reused password compromises every account that shares it.

Two-factor authentication adds a second verification layer beyond passwords. Enable it on all accounts that offer it, particularly email, financial services, social media, and any account having sensitive information. Use authenticator applications rather than SMS-based verification when available, as SMS codes are vulnerable to interception through SIM-swapping attacks where criminals transfer your phone number to a device they control.

Keep all software updated on all devices. Operating systems, applications, browsers, and firmware all receive security updates that patch known vulnerabilities. Attackers actively target known vulnerabilities in outdated software because they are well-documented and exploitation tools are readily available. Automatic updates should be enabled wherever possible.

Use a virtual private network when connecting to public Wi-Fi networks. A VPN encrypts your internet traffic, preventing others on the same network from intercepting your data. Public networks in coffee shops, airports, hotels, and other shared spaces are common attack vectors because traffic on these networks is typically unencrypted and visible to anyone with basic interception tools.

Install and keep reputable antivirus and anti-malware software. While no software provides complete protection, these tools detect and block known threats, scan downloads and attachments, and watch system behavior for indicators of compromise. Keep virus definitions updated to ensure protection against newly identified threats.

Back up important data regularly to a separate location, whether an external drive or a cloud storage service. Backups protect against ransomware, which becomes ineffective if you can restore your data from an uncompromised backup. They also protect against hardware failure, accidental deletion, and other data loss scenarios. Maintain at least one backup that is not continuously connected to your primary device, as some ransomware specifically targets connected backup drives.

Protecting Your Privacy

Privacy protection requires understanding what information you generate, who collects it, and how it is used. Every online interaction produces data. Websites track your browsing behavior through cookies and other tracking technologies. Applications collect usage data, location information, contact lists, and other device data. Social media platforms analyze your interactions to build detailed behavioral profiles used for targeted advertising.

Review and configure privacy settings on all devices, applications, and online accounts. Default settings typically maximize data collection. Disable location services for applications that do not require it. Restrict access to your contacts, photos, and other device data to only those applications with a legitimate need. Review application permissions periodically, as updates sometimes add new data collection that requires fresh consent.

Be deliberate about the information you share online. Every piece of personal information you post, your location, daily routines, travel plans, financial details, relationship status, and finding information, can potentially be aggregated to build a comprehensive profile. This information can be used for targeted advertising, social engineering attacks, identity theft, or physical security threats such as burglary of homes identified as unoccupied through travel posts.

Understand that free online services monetize your data. When a product is free, your attention and personal information are typically the product being sold. This does not necessarily mean you should avoid free services, but you should understand the exchange you are making and configure privacy settings to limit data collection to the extent possible.

Review your digital footprint periodically. Search for your name and review what information about you is publicly accessible. Request removal of personal information from data broker sites that compile and sell personal data. Monitor your credit reports for unauthorized accounts, which may show identity theft. Proactive monitoring enables early detection and faster response to privacy compromises.

Developing Sustainable Security Habits

Cybersecurity is not a one-time configuration but an ongoing practice. Threats evolve continuously, and the protections that are adequate today may be insufficient tomorrow. Developing sustainable habits is more effective than implementing perfect security once and neglecting it afterward.

Monitor your accounts regularly for unauthorized activity. Review bank and credit card statements for unfamiliar charges. Check email account activity logs for logins from unfamiliar locations or devices. Review social media account settings for authorized applications or sessions you do not recognize. Early detection of unauthorized access limits the damage an attacker can cause.

Stay informed about emerging threats. Cybersecurity news sources report on new attack methods, major breaches, and newly discovered vulnerabilities. You do not need to follow this topic intensively, but periodic awareness of significant developments enables you to adjust your practices accordingly. Major breaches affecting services you use should prompt immediate password changes and security reviews.

Apply the principle of least privilege to your digital life. Grant applications, services, and people only the minimum access they need to function. Do not give administrator access when standard access suffices. Do not share credentials with others. Do not grant applications access to data they do not need for their core function. Limiting access limits the potential damage from any single compromise.

Treat cybersecurity as an investment rather than an inconvenience. The time spent on password management, software updates, privacy configuration, and security awareness is minimal compared to the time, financial cost, and stress needed to recover from identity theft, ransomware, or a compromised financial account. Prevention is consistently less expensive than remediation.

Chapter 30: Online Job Search Strategies

Introduction

The job search process has moved predominantly online. Job postings, applications, resume submissions, initial screenings, and often interviews themselves all occur through digital platforms. Navigating this process effectively requires specific skills: creating application materials that pass both automated screening systems and human review, building a professional digital presence that supports your candidacy, using job platforms strategically, and keeping organization throughout what can be a prolonged and complex process.

The online job market presents both opportunities and challenges. The volume of available positions is greater than at any earlier point, but so is the competition. Automated applicant tracking systems filter applications before a human ever sees them. Your digital presence is evaluated alongside your formal application materials. Scams targeting job seekers are common. Approaching the online job search with strategy, preparation, and awareness significantly improves your outcomes.

This chapter covers creating effective application materials, building a professional online presence, using job platforms strategically, keeping organization during your search, and protecting yourself from job search scams.

Creating Effective Application Materials

Your resume is typically the first document a potential employer encounters. In the online application environment, it must perform two functions: it must pass through applicant tracking systems that screen for specific keywords and qualifications, and it must communicate your value clearly to the human reviewers who evaluate candidates that pass initial screening.

Structure your resume clearly with consistent formatting. Use a clean, professional layout with clear section headings for contact information, professional summary, work experience, education, and skills. Use standard section names that applicant tracking systems recognize. Avoid elaborate graphics, tables, columns, or unusual formatting that may not parse correctly through automated systems.

Tailor your resume to each position. Review the job description carefully and align your experience and skills with the specific requirements listed. Use language from the job description where it accurately describes your experience, as applicant tracking systems often screen for specific terminology. This does not mean fabricating experience but rather framing your genuine qualifications in terms that match what the employer is looking for.

Quantify achievements wherever possible. Stating that you increased sales, improved efficiency, or managed projects is vague. Stating that you increased sales by twenty-three percent, reduced processing time from five days to two, or managed a team of eight people completing a six-month project provides concrete evidence of your capabilities. Specific numbers give reviewers tangible information to evaluate.

Cover letters should complement rather than repeat your resume. Use the cover letter to explain why you are interested in the specific position and organization, how your experience prepares you for the role's particular challenges, and what you would bring beyond what your resume shows. A compelling cover letter shows that you have researched the organization and thought carefully about the fit between your capabilities and their needs.

Building a Professional Online Presence

Employers research candidates online. Your digital presence functions as an extension of your application materials, providing other information about your professional identity, communication abilities, and judgment. Managing this presence deliberately ensures it supports rather than undermines your job search.

LinkedIn is the primary professional networking platform and merits particular attention. Create a complete profile with a professional photo, descriptive headline that communicates your professional identity beyond just a job title, detailed experience descriptions with accomplishments, and a summary that articulates your professional value and goals. A well-maintained LinkedIn profile serves as a living professional document that recruiters actively search.

Engage on LinkedIn by sharing relevant industry content, commenting thoughtfully on posts in your field, and publishing your own insights when you have valuable perspectives to offer. Active engagement increases your visibility to recruiters and shows professional interest and knowledge that a static profile alone cannot convey.

If your work produces visible outputs, whether writing, design, code, research, or other creative or technical products, create a portfolio website or use proper platforms to showcase your best work. A portfolio provides evidence of your capabilities that a resume can only describe. Even a simple, well-organized collection of work samples significantly strengthens your candidacy for roles where demonstrable skill is valued.

Audit all your public-facing social media from an employer's perspective. Remove or restrict content that would create a negative professional impression. Ensure that your public profiles across platforms present a consistent, professional image. This does not require dropping all personal content but does require ensuring that nothing publicly visible would give a reasonable employer pause about your judgment or professionalism.

Using Job Platforms Strategically

Major job platforms including, Indeed, LinkedIn, Glassdoor, and industry-specific job boards aggregate thousands of positions. Using these platforms effectively requires more than browsing listings. Configure detailed search filters to focus on positions matching your qualifications, experience level, location preferences, and salary requirements. Set up email alerts for searches that match your criteria so new listings reach you promptly.

Research employers before applying. Company websites, employee reviews on platforms like Glassdoor, news coverage, and social media presence provide insight into organizational culture, financial stability, growth trajectory, and employee satisfaction. This research helps you prioritize applications toward organizations where you are most likely to thrive and enables you to customize application materials effectively.

Networking is still the most effective job search strategy even in the digital era. Many positions are filled through professional connections before they are publicly posted. Informational interviews, where you request brief conversations with professionals in your field to learn about their work and industry, build relationships that can lead to opportunities. Alumni networks, professional associations, and industry events, both in-person and virtual, provide more networking channels.

Follow up appropriately after submitting applications. A brief, professional follow-up email approximately one week after applying expresses continued interest and can move your application to active consideration. Keep follow-ups concise, professional, and respectful of the hiring team's time. If no response follows a reasonable period and a follow-up, move your attention to other opportunities rather than sending multiple messages.

Staying Organized and Avoiding Scams

An organized job search process produces better results and less stress than a chaotic one. Track every application in a spreadsheet or dedicated application tracking tool, recording the company name, position title, date applied, application method, contact information, and any follow-up dates. This prevents duplicate applications, ensures prompt follow-up, and provides a clear picture of your search progress.

Job search scams are prevalent on online platforms. Common indicators include positions that promise unusually high compensation for minimal qualifications, employers that request payment for training materials or background checks, job offers extended without interviews, requests for personal financial information early in the process, and communications from generic email addresses rather than corporate domains. Legitimate employers do not charge applicants fees, do not request banking information before hiring, and conduct substantive interviews before extending offers.

Research any company that contacts you before providing personal information or attending interviews. Verify that the company exists, has a legitimate web presence, and that the position matches information on their official website. Search for the company name combined with terms like "scam" or "reviews" to find reported issues. Trust your judgment: if an opportunity seems disproportionately attractive for the requirements, it likely is.

Maintain momentum throughout the search process. Job searching can be discouraging, particularly when responses are slow or rejections accumulate. Establish a sustainable routine that includes a specific number of applications per week, regular networking activities, and ongoing skill development. Treat the job search as a project to be managed rather than an open-ended waiting period. Continue developing relevant skills through online courses, certifications, volunteer work, or personal projects during your search. These activities strengthen your candidacy while providing productive focus during gaps between applications.

The Road Ahead

Online job search is a skill set that improves with practice and strategic thinking. Creating strong application materials, building a professional digital presence, using platforms efficiently, supporting organization, and exercising caution together form an effective approach. The digital job market rewards candidates who approach it with the same preparation and professionalism they would bring to the positions they look for. The habits you develop during your job search, including attention to detail, strategic communication, networking, and persistence, are the same habits that contribute to professional success once employed.

Section 5: Communication

Communication ability decides professional outcomes more directly than most technical skills. The capacity to express ideas clearly, listen effectively, speak persuasively, build professional relationships, and understand your own strengths shapes every interaction that matters: job interviews, workplace collaboration, client relationships, negotiations, leadership, and career advancement.

Most people overestimate their communication competence. Familiarity with casual conversation does not translate to professional communication effectiveness. Speaking clearly under pressure, writing concisely for professional audiences, listening with genuine attention, resolving conflicts constructively, presenting ideas to groups, building networks of professional relationships, and articulating your own value proposition are distinct skills that require deliberate development.

This section addresses four areas of communication competence. Effective communication covers the foundational skills of active listening, clear expression, nonverbal awareness, professional writing, and conflict resolution. Public speaking addresses preparation, delivery, anxiety management, and continuous improvement in presentation contexts. Networking examines how to build and keep professional relationships that create mutual value over time. Finding personal strengths provides a framework for understanding your capabilities and interests and communicating them effectively in professional contexts.

Each of these skills is learnable and improvable through practice. None needs a particular personality type. Effective communicators are not born with innate talent. They develop competence through understanding principles, applying them deliberately, and refining their approach based on feedback and outcomes.

Chapter 31: Effective Communication

Introduction

Effective communication is the ability to convey information, ideas, and intentions clearly while accurately receiving and interpreting what others communicate. In professional environments, communication quality directly affects team performance, project outcomes, relationship quality, and career progression. Miscommunication causes missed deadlines, duplicated work, damaged relationships, and lost opportunities. Strong communication prevents these problems and creates the trust, clarity, and coordination that productive work requires.

Communication competence encompasses multiple distinct skills: listening attentively, speaking clearly and purposefully, reading nonverbal signals, writing professionally, managing difficult conversations, and adapting your communication style to different audiences and contexts. Each skill can be developed independently, and improvement in any area produces immediate practical benefits.

Active Listening

Listening is the most undervalued communication skill. Most people listen passively, waiting for their turn to speak rather than fully processing what the other person is communicating. Active listening requires focused attention on the speaker, conscious effort to understand their message, and deliberate withholding of your own response until you have fully received theirs.

Active listening involves several specific practices. Maintain attention on the speaker without mentally preparing your response while they talk. Observe nonverbal cues including tone, facial expression, and body language, which often convey information that words alone do not. Ask clarifying questions to ensure correct understanding: restating what you heard in your own words and asking whether your interpretation is correct prevents misunderstandings before they cause problems. Avoid interrupting, even when you believe you already understand the point being made.

In professional settings, active listening builds trust and improves outcomes. When colleagues and supervisors feel genuinely heard, they communicate more openly, share concerns earlier, and collaborate more willingly. Active listening also improves your own decision-making because you run with more complete and correct information. The investment of attention required by active listening consistently produces returns in relationship quality and work effectiveness.

Speaking with Clarity and Purpose

Clear verbal communication requires organizing your thoughts before expressing them. Decide your core message before you begin speaking. State it directly, support it with relevant detail, and avoid tangential information that dilutes your point. Concise communication respects your audience's time and attention while ensuring your message is understood.

Adapt your communication to your audience. The vocabulary, level of detail, tone, and formality right for a conversation with your supervisor differ from those proper for a discussion with peers or a presentation to clients. This is not about being inauthentic but about ensuring your message is received effectively by the specific people you are addressing. Technical language that communicates efficiently with specialists confuses generalist audiences. Casual language that works among peers may undermine credibility with senior leadership.

Clarification is a strength, not a weakness. Confirming your understanding of instructions, expectations, or discussed decisions prevents errors that waste far more time than the clarification itself. Phrases such as "I want to confirm I understand correctly" or "Let me restate what I heard to make sure we are aligned" show professionalism and prevent the costly misunderstandings that assumptions produce.

Filler words and verbal habits such as "um," "like," and "you know" reduce the clarity and perceived confidence of your communication. While occasional filler is normal, excessive use distracts from your message. Awareness is the first step toward reduction. Recording yourself during practice presentations or asking trusted colleagues for feedback helps show patterns you may not notice independently.

Nonverbal Communication

Nonverbal communication, including body language, facial expressions, eye contact, posture, and tone of voice, conveys significant information that either reinforces or contradicts your spoken words. Research consistently shows that when verbal and nonverbal messages conflict, people trust the nonverbal signal. Saying you are enthusiastic while your posture, expression, and tone convey disinterest undermines your credibility regardless of your words.

In face-to-face interactions, keep proper eye contact to signal engagement and confidence. Open body posture, facing the speaker with uncrossed arms, communicates receptivity. Nodding appropriately signals understanding and attention. These behaviors are not performative. They help genuine connection and signal respect for the interaction.

In virtual communication, nonverbal dynamics change but do not disappear. Looking at the camera rather than the screen simulates eye contact. Ensuring adequate lighting and a clean background presents professionalism. Minimizing visible distractions and keeping attentive posture communicate the same respect for the interaction that physical presence would.

Tone carries particular weight in written communication, where body language and facial expression are absent. Without these contextual cues, written messages are often interpreted more negatively than intended. Professional written communication benefits from explicit clarity about intent, proper courtesy language, and careful review before sending. Rereading a message from the recipient's perspective before sending it catches tone problems that are obvious to a reader but invisible to the writer.

Professional Writing

Professional writing prioritizes clarity, conciseness, and proper tone. Emails, messages, reports, and other written communications should convey their essential information efficiently. State your purpose in the first sentence or paragraph. Provide necessary context and detail without unnecessary elaboration. Use clear structure, including paragraph breaks and descriptive subject lines for emails, which enables readers to find relevant information quickly.

Proofread all professional communications before sending. Spelling errors, grammatical mistakes, and unclear phrasing undermine your credibility and can cause genuine misunderstandings. This applies to brief emails as well as formal documents. The few seconds needed to review a message before sending it are consistently worthwhile.

Match the formality of your writing to the context. Internal team messages may be relatively casual. Communications with clients, senior leadership, or external contacts typically need more formal language and structure. When uncertain about the proper level of formality, err toward more formal. It is easier to become more casual once a relationship is proven than to recover from a first impression of unprofessionalism.

Conflict Resolution

Conflict is inevitable in professional environments. Differing priorities, miscommunications, resource constraints, and personality differences all generate disagreement. Effective conflict resolution focuses on finding and addressing the underlying issue rather than winning the argument.

Use statements that describe your experience rather than attributing blame. Expressing that you were confused by a timeline change communicates the problem without provoking defensiveness in the way that accusing someone of not communicating does. This distinction matters because defensive reactions escalate conflicts while collaborative framing moves toward resolution.

Listen to the other party's perspective fully before responding. Acknowledge their concerns, even when you disagree. Understanding their position does not require agreeing with it, but it shows respect and often reveals information that changes how you view the situation. Many conflicts stem from incomplete information on one or both sides rather than from genuinely irreconcilable positions.

Focus on solutions rather than showing fault. Once both parties understand the issue, direct the conversation toward what can be done going forward. What changes would prevent this problem from recurring? What actions will address the current situation? Resolution-focused conversations produce better outcomes and stronger working relationships than blame-focused ones.

The Road Ahead

Communication is a skill set that improves continuously with deliberate practice. Every professional interaction, whether a brief email, a team meeting, a difficult conversation, or a routine check-in, is an opportunity to practice listening more carefully, expressing yourself more clearly, reading nonverbal signals more accurately, and managing disagreements more constructively. The cumulative effect of these improvements shapes how others perceive you, how effectively you collaborate, and how quickly you advance professionally.

Chapter 32: Public Speaking

Introduction

Public speaking is the ability to communicate ideas effectively to a group. It is consistently ranked among the most valuable professional skills and among the most common sources of anxiety. Both of these facts are relevant: public speaking ability provides disproportionate professional advantage precisely because most people avoid developing it. Those who invest in this skill distinguish themselves in meetings, presentations, interviews, and any context were communicating to a group decides outcomes.

Public speaking anxiety is normal and manageable. It does not show lack of ability. Many accomplished speakers experience nervousness before presentations. The difference between effective and ineffective speakers is not the presence or absence of anxiety but the preparation, techniques, and practice that enable performance despite it. This chapter covers preparation, delivery, anxiety management, and the iterative improvement process that builds competence over time.

Preparation

Preparation is the single most important factor in public speaking success. Thorough preparation reduces anxiety, improves delivery, and ensures your message is coherent and compelling. Insufficient preparation is the cause of most poor presentations, not lack of natural talent.

Begin by analyzing your audience. Their knowledge level, interests, expectations, and relationship to your topic should decide your content, vocabulary, level of detail, and tone. A technical presentation to specialists requires different preparation than an overview for general audiences. Understanding what your audience already knows prevents both condescension and confusion.

Organize your content around a clear structure. Every effective presentation has a defined purpose, a logical progression of ideas, and a clear conclusion. Find your core message, the single idea you want your audience to remember, and ensure every element of your presentation supports it. Supporting points should follow a logical sequence that builds understanding incrementally. Transitions between sections should be explicit so your audience can follow the structure of your argument.

Know your material thoroughly rather than memorizing a script. Memorization produces rigid delivery that collapses when you lose your place or face unexpected interruptions. Understanding your material deeply enables you to present it conversationally, adapt to audience reactions, answer questions confidently, and recover smoothly from disruptions. Practice by explaining your content in different ways until you can present the key ideas naturally regardless of the specific words you use.

Prepare for technical failures. Equipment malfunctions, software problems, and display issues occur regularly. Having a backup plan, whether printed notes, a secondary device, or the ability to present without visual aids, prevents a technical problem from becoming a presentation failure. Evaluate all equipment in advance when possible.

Visual Aids

Visual aids should support your message, not substitute for it. Slides that have your entire presentation in text form serve no purpose beyond making the speaker unnecessary. Effective slides use images, graphs, and minimal text to reinforce key points while you provide the explanation, context, and narrative verbally.

Design slides for clarity and readability. Use high-contrast text, large font sizes, and simple layouts. Each slide should convey one idea. Avoid cluttered slides that force your audience to read rather than listen. If your audience is reading your slides, they are not listening to you, and you are no longer presenting but rather displaying a document.

Never read directly from slides. Your slides are reference points for your audience, not a script for you. Looking at the screen rather than the audience breaks the connection that makes presentations engaging. Use speaker notes if you need prompts and keep eye contact with your audience while delivering your content.

Delivery and Engagement

Effective delivery combines vocal variety, purposeful body language, and audience engagement. Speak at a measured pace. Nervous speakers commonly accelerate, making their content harder to follow and conveying anxiety rather than confidence. Deliberately slowing your pace, particularly at the beginning of a presentation and when making important points, improves comprehension and projects composure.

Use pauses strategically. A pause after a key statement gives your audience time to absorb the point and signals that what you just said matters. Pauses feel longer for the speaker than for the audience. What feels like an uncomfortable silence to you typically appears like confident delivery to your listeners.

Vary your vocal tone and volume to keep audience attention and emphasize important content. Monotone delivery causes audiences to disengage regardless of content quality. Lowering your voice draws listeners in. Increasing volume emphasizes critical points. Vocal variety keeps your audience attentive and makes your content more memorable.

Body language reinforces or undermines your spoken message. Stand with balanced posture and use deliberate hand gestures to emphasize points. Avoid repetitive movements such as pacing, swaying, or fidgeting, which distract from your content and signal nervousness. Eye contact with different sections of your audience builds connection and conveys confidence. In large venues, direct your gaze to different areas of the room rather than fixing on one spot or staring at your notes.

Engage your audience actively. Ask questions, invite responses, or use examples that connect your content to their experience. Audiences who feel involved in a presentation pay closer attention and keep more information than those who passively receive a monologue. Even brief moments of interaction shift the dynamic from lecture to conversation.

Managing Anxiety

Speaking anxiety manifests physically through increased heart rate, shallow breathing, sweating, trembling, and dry mouth. These are normal stress responses that can be managed through specific techniques. Deep breathing before and during your presentation activates the parasympathetic nervous system, counteracting the physiological stress response. Inhale slowly for four counts, hold for four counts, and exhale for four counts. Several cycles of this pattern measurably reduce anxiety symptoms.

Physical preparation also helps. Arrive early to familiarize yourself with the space and evaluate equipment. Stand where you will present and visualize the experience going well. These actions reduce the novelty of the situation, which is a significant anxiety trigger. The more familiar the environment feels before you begin, the less anxious you will be when you start.

Reframe anxiety as energy rather than show of incapacity. The physiological symptoms of anxiety and excitement are nearly identical. Interpreting your racing heart as preparation for performance rather than a signal of danger changes your psychological relationship with the sensation without requiring you to cut it. Most audiences cannot detect your internal anxiety. The nervousness you feel is far more visible to you than to your listeners.

Experience is the most effective anxiety reducer. Each presentation you deliver builds familiarity with the situation and evidence that you can perform competently. Seek opportunities to speak in low-stakes environments, such as team meetings, small group discussions, or volunteer organizations, to build confidence before facing high-stakes presentations. Competence develops through repetition, and with competence comes genuine confidence.

Continuous Improvement

Seek feedback after every presentation. Ask trusted colleagues or audience members what was effective and what could be improved. Specific feedback, such as noting that your pace was too fast during the middle section or that a particular example was especially clear, provides actionable information that general praise or criticism does not.

Record yourself when possible. Reviewing recordings reveals habits, both positive and negative, that you cannot see while presenting. Common discoveries include filler word frequency, pacing patterns, eye contact tendencies, and gestures you were unaware of making. This self-observation accelerates improvement because it provides objective evidence of your actual delivery rather than your feeling of it.

Public speaking competence develops incrementally. Each presentation builds on the earlier one. Accept that early presentations will be imperfect and that improvement comes through consistent practice rather than avoiding opportunities until you feel ready. Waiting until you feel confident to speak publicly inverts the actual process: confidence follows competence, and competence develops through practice.

Chapter 33: Networking

Introduction

Networking is the deliberate process of building and supporting professional relationships that provide mutual value over time. It is one of the most effective career development activities available, yet it is often misunderstood as self-serving, superficial, or relevant only to extroverted personalities. In practice, effective networking is about genuine relationship building: offering value to others, supporting connections consistently, and creating a network of people who support each other's professional growth.

Research consistently shows that professional networks are among the strongest predictors of career outcomes. A significant percentage of positions are filled through referrals and professional connections rather than public job postings. Beyond job access, networks provide mentorship, industry knowledge, collaborative opportunities, and perspective that you cannot obtain independently. Investing in professional relationships is not optional supplementary activity but a core part of career development.

Building Your Professional Identity

Before engaging in networking, clarify what you offer and what you look for. Your professional identity encompasses your skills, experience, values, areas of expertise, and the specific value you provide in professional contexts. Articulating this clearly, both to yourself and to others, enables genuine and productive networking conversations rather than vague exchanges that produce no lasting connection.

Develop a concise professional introduction that communicates who you are, what you do or are working toward, and what interests you professionally. This is not a rehearsed sales pitch but a clear, natural description that enables others to understand your background and find potential points of connection. Practice articulating your professional identity until it feels natural rather than scripted.

Your online professional presence, particularly on LinkedIn, functions as your persistent professional introduction. Ensure your profile accurately reflects your experience, skills, and professional interests. A complete profile with a professional photo, descriptive headline, detailed experience section, and thoughtful summary enables people you meet to learn more about you after first contact and allows recruiters and potential collaborators to find you through searches.

Making Meaningful Connections

Effective networking occurs in many contexts: industry conferences, professional associations, alumni events, community organizations, workplace interactions, and online platforms. Each context offers different opportunities and requires slightly different approaches, but the fundamental principle stays consistent: focus on genuine connection rather than transactional exchange.

In-person networking events can feel uncomfortable, particularly if you are naturally introverted. A practical approach is to prepare several open-ended questions that invite substantive conversation. Asking what someone is currently working on, what brought them to the event, or what trends they are seeing in their field produces more meaningful exchanges than generic pleasantries. Genuine curiosity about other people's work and perspectives is the most effective networking skill regardless of personality type.

Online networking extends your reach beyond geographic and event-based limitations. Engage thoughtfully with content posted by professionals in your field. Share your own insights, comment substantively on others' posts, and take part in professional group discussions. When reaching out to new contacts, personalize your message by referencing specific shared interests, mutual connections, or content they have shared. Generic connection requests are easily ignored. Specific, thoughtful outreach shows genuine interest.

Informational interviews, where you request a brief conversation with a professional to learn about their field, role, or career path, are among the most effective networking tools available. Most professionals are willing to share their experience when approached respectfully and with specific, thoughtful questions. These conversations provide industry knowledge, practical career advice, and relationship foundations that can develop into ongoing professional connections.

Volunteering and community involvement offer natural networking opportunities in contexts that feel less transactional than formal events. Working alongside others toward shared goals builds genuine relationships and shows your character, work ethic, and skills in ways that conversation alone cannot. Many professionals report that their most valuable connections originated from volunteer work, community organizations, or collaborative projects rather than from formal networking events.

Maintaining and Strengthening Relationships

Building connections is only valuable if you support them. Networking is not a one-time activity but an ongoing practice of relationship maintenance. Following up after first meetings with a brief message referencing your conversation and expressing appreciation for the connection sets up the relationship. Without follow-up, most first contacts are forgotten within weeks.

Maintain your network through periodic, genuine engagement. Share articles or opportunities relevant to your contacts' interests. Congratulate professional achievements. Check in periodically without needing anything specific. These small actions support relationship warmth and keep you present in your contacts' awareness. When opportunities arise on either side, active relationships produce action. Dormant ones do not.

Provide value before seeking it. Recommend people for opportunities, make introductions between contacts who might benefit from knowing each other, share relevant information, and offer help when your skills or knowledge are relevant to someone's challenge. People who consistently contribute to their network's success build reputations that generate reciprocal generosity. Those who only reach out when they need something build reputations that close doors.

Follow through on commitments consistently. If you promise to send information, make an introduction, or follow up on a conversation, do it promptly. Reliability is a distinguishing characteristic in professional relationships. In an environment where many people do not follow through on casual commitments, consistent reliability makes you someone others actively want in their network.

The Road Ahead

Networking is relationship building with professional intentionality. It requires genuine interest in other people, consistent effort to support connections, willingness to provide value before receiving it, and reliability in following through on commitments. These are not personality traits limited to extroverts but practices accessible to anyone willing to engage deliberately. The professional network you build over time becomes one of your most valuable career assets, providing access to opportunities, knowledge, support, and perspective that no individual can develop alone.

Chapter 34: Identifying Personal Strengths

Introduction

Understanding your strengths and interests is prerequisite to effective career planning, professional communication, and purposeful decision-making. Without clarity about what you do well and what motivates you, career choices become reactive rather than strategic, professional messaging becomes generic rather than compelling, and decisions about education, training, and opportunity pursuit lack grounding in self-knowledge.

Finding personal strengths is not a one-time exercise completed through a single assessment or moment of reflection. It is an ongoing process of observation, experimentation, and refinement that develops throughout your career. Your strengths become clearer through varied experience, feedback from others, and honest self-assessment. This chapter provides a framework for that process: methods for finding your existing strengths, approaches for exploring your interests, and strategies for connecting both to career possibilities.

Recognizing Your Strengths

Strengths are capabilities where you consistently perform well and that feel natural or energizing to apply. They differ from skills, which are learned competencies that may or may not align with natural aptitude. You can develop skills in areas that are not natural strengths, but you perform most effectively and sustainably in areas where developed skills align with underlying strengths.

Find your strengths by examining patterns across your experiences. Consider moments when you performed at your best, when work felt engaging rather than draining, when others sought your help or recognized your contribution, and when you produced results that exceeded your own expectations. Common themes across these experiences reveal underlying strengths. If you consistently excel at explaining complex ideas to others, communication and translation of complexity are likely strengths. If you naturally organize chaotic situations into structured plans, strategic thinking and organizational capability are strengths.

Formal assessment tools provide added perspective. The Myers-Briggs Type Indicator, CliftonStrengths assessment, Holland Code career interest inventory, and similar instruments offer structured frameworks for understanding your tendencies, preferences, and aptitudes. These tools are most useful when treated as starting points for reflection rather than definitive categorizations. No assessment captures the full complexity of an individual, but well-designed instruments find patterns that merit further exploration.

External feedback is invaluable for finding strengths that are invisible to you precisely because they come naturally. Ask people who have collaborated with you, supervised you, or known you in various contexts what they consider your greatest strengths and when they have seen you at your best. Others often see capabilities in you that you take for granted because they feel effortless. What feels easy to you may be genuinely difficult for others, and recognizing this asymmetry is essential for correct self-assessment.

Exploring Your Interests

Interests show what engages your attention and motivation. They signal areas where you are most likely to invest the sustained effort that produces ability and satisfaction. Interests and strengths often overlap but are not identical. You may be interested in areas where you are not yet strong, and you may have strengths in areas that do not particularly interest you. The most fulfilling and effective career paths typically combine both: work that uses your strengths in an area that genuinely interests you.

Explore interests actively rather than waiting for clarity to appear. Take courses in subjects that intrigue you. Volunteer in different contexts. Accept projects outside your usual scope. Attend talks, read widely, and engage with people working in diverse fields. Each experience provides data about what engages you and what does not. Both positive and negative discoveries are valuable. Dropping options that do not interest you narrows the field as effectively as finding ones that do.

Distinguish between core interests and surface-level attraction. A fascination with a field's visible outputs does not necessarily show interest in the daily work that produces them. Before committing to a career direction, investigate what the actual work involves through informational interviews, job shadowing, internships, or detailed research into typical responsibilities and working conditions. Alignment between your interests and the reality of the work, not just its public image, predicts sustained satisfaction.

Recognize that interests evolve. What engages you at twenty may differ from what motivates you at thirty or forty. This evolution is normal and healthy. Career planning should accommodate development rather than assuming permanent preferences. Build a foundation of transferable skills and professional relationships that enable you to pursue new interests as they appear rather than locking yourself into a single trajectory.

Connecting Strengths and Interests to Career Possibilities

The intersection of your strengths and interests defines the career space where you are most likely to excel and find satisfaction. Map your identified strengths against your confirmed interests and research career paths that require both. Online occupational databases, industry publications, and informational interviews with professionals in relevant fields provide concrete information about which careers align with your particular combination.

Research career paths thoroughly before committing resources. Investigate educational requirements, typical career progression, compensation ranges, working conditions, demand trends, and geographic considerations. Understand not just what a role involves today but how the field is evolving and what skills will be valuable in the future. Informed career decisions account for trajectory as well as current conditions.

Gain direct experience through internships, part-time work, volunteer roles, or personal projects in areas that interest you. Direct experience provides information that research alone cannot: whether you enjoy the actual work, how well your strengths apply in practice, and whether the working environment suits your preferences. Even brief exposure can confirm or redirect your career thinking more effectively than extended deliberation without experience.

Recognize that career development is iterative rather than linear. Few people find their ideal career path before beginning it. Most discover their direction through a series of experiences that progressively clarify their strengths, interests, and values. Each position, project, and professional experience provides information that refines your understanding of where you fit and what you want. Approach career development as an ongoing experiment rather than a permanent decision and give yourself permission to adjust course as you learn more about yourself and the professional landscape.

The Road Ahead

Finding your strengths and interests is foundational work that informs every later career decision. It decides what opportunities you pursue, how you present yourself professionally, where you invest your development effort, and how satisfied you are with your professional life. This identification is not a single event but a continuous process of self-observation, external feedback, active experimentation, and honest reflection. The clarity you develop about your own capabilities and motivations is one of the most valuable career assets you can build, and it improves with every new experience and honest assessment.

Section 6: Developing A Career Plan

Career development requires intentional planning. Without a structured approach, career decisions become reactive, driven by whatever opportunity appears next rather than by deliberate strategy aligned with your strengths, interests, and long-term goals. A career plan provides direction without requiring permanent commitment to a single path. It sets up priorities, defines actionable steps, and creates a framework for evaluating opportunities as they arise.

Most people enter the workforce without a coherent career strategy. They accept available positions, respond to immediate financial pressures, and discover their professional direction through trial and error rather than deliberate exploration. While some degree of experimentation is inevitable and valuable, approaching career development with intentionality produces better outcomes than passivity. People who plan their careers report higher job satisfaction, faster advancement, and greater alignment between their work and their values.

This section addresses three phases of career development. Building a career plan covers self-assessment, research, goal setting, and the creation of a flexible plan that guides your decisions. Mastering the job search addresses the practical skills of finding, applying for, and securing positions effectively. Long-term career success examines the habits and practices that sustain professional growth, build reputation, and enable adaptation across a career spanning decades.

Career planning is not a single event but an ongoing process. Your plan will evolve as you gain experience, develop new skills, and refine your understanding of what you want from your professional life. The framework presented here provides structure for that evolution, ensuring that each career decision builds on the earlier one rather than occurring in isolation.

Chapter 35: Building a Career Plan

Introduction

A career plan is a structured approach to professional development that connects your current position to your long-term aims through defined goals and actionable steps. It does not require certainty about your ultimate destination. It requires honest self-assessment, informed research, specific goals, and willingness to adjust as you learn more about yourself and the professional landscape. A flexible career plan provides direction during periods of uncertainty and a basis for evaluating opportunities when they arise.

Self-Assessment

Effective career planning begins with understanding what you bring to the professional world and what you want from it. The self-assessment process covered in Chapter 34 provides the foundation: finding your strengths, skills, interests, values, and working preferences. This information decides which career paths are likely to produce both competence and satisfaction.

Distinguish between skills you have developed and strengths that come naturally. Skills can be acquired for any career path through training and practice. Strengths are areas where you learn faster, perform more consistently, and sustain effort more easily. Careers that use your natural strengths while allowing you to develop complementary skills produce the best long-term outcomes.

Clarify your values about work. Some people prioritize income and financial security. Others value autonomy, creative expression, social impact, intellectual challenge, work-life balance, or geographic flexibility. There is no universally correct set of priorities. Understanding your own values prevents the common mistake of pursuing career paths that look impressive externally but do not satisfy your actual priorities. A high-paying position that violates your core values produces dissatisfaction regardless of compensation.

Career Research

Once you understand your strengths, skills, and values, research careers that align with them. Use occupational databases, industry publications, professional association resources, and job postings to understand what specific careers involve on a daily basis. Investigate educational requirements, typical career progression, compensation ranges, job market demand, and working conditions. This research replaces assumptions with evidence.

Informational interviews are among the most effective research tools available. Request brief conversations with professionals working in fields that interest you. Ask about their daily responsibilities, how they entered the field, what they find rewarding and challenging, and what advice they would give someone considering the path. These conversations provide perspective that no written resource can replicate: honest, personal accounts of what the work actually involves.

Seek direct experience when possible. Internships, part-time positions, volunteer roles, freelance projects, and job shadowing provide firsthand exposure to career now

fields. Direct experience is the most reliable way to decide whether a career path suits you because it reveals the reality of the work rather than only its public image. Even brief exposure can confirm or redirect your planning more effectively than extended deliberation.

Setting Goals and Creating a Plan

Define your long-term career vision based on your self-assessment and research. This vision does not need to specify a single job title. It should describe the type of work, the level of responsibility, the working conditions, and the impact you want to achieve. A vision such as leading technical projects in a growing company, running an independent consulting practice, or working in public health policy provides sufficient direction for planning without requiring premature specificity.

Break your long-term vision into medium-term goals spanning one to five years and short-term goals achievable within months. Apply the SMART framework: make each goal Specific, Measurable, Achievable, Relevant, and Time-bound. Completing a certification by a specific date, gaining experience in a particular skill area within six months, or securing a position at a target level within two years are actionable goals that convert vision into progress.

Create a timeline that sequences your goals logically. Find dependencies: which goals must be achieved before others become possible. Find the education, training, experience, and connections needed for each step. Build these requirements into your plan as their own sub-goals. A detailed plan with clear milestones enables you to track progress, keep momentum, and show when adjustments are needed.

Review and update your plan regularly. Quarterly reviews allow you to assess progress, incorporate new information, and adjust goals based on what you have learned. Career plans that stay static become irrelevant as circumstances change. Plans that evolve with your experience and understanding remain useful throughout your career.

The Road Ahead

A career plan is a living document, not a binding contract. Its value lies in providing structure for decisions that would otherwise be made ad hoc. By grounding your plan in honest self-assessment, thorough research, and specific goals, you create a framework that guides your professional development while staying flexible enough to accommodate the unexpected opportunities and changes of direction that characterize every career.

Chapter 36: Mastering the Job Search

Introduction

The job search is a distinct skill set separate from the professional skills needed to perform well once employed. It requires creating effective application materials, using digital platforms strategically, networking purposefully, and performing well in interviews. Many qualified candidates receive fewer opportunities than less qualified ones simply because their job search execution is weaker. Developing competence in the job search process itself significantly affects career outcomes.

Using Online Platforms Effectively

Online job platforms aggregate thousands of positions across industries and locations. Sites such as Indeed, LinkedIn, Glassdoor, and industry-specific job boards are primary channels for both job seekers and employers. Use these platforms strategically rather than passively. Configure detailed search filters to focus on positions matching your qualifications, experience level, and preferences. Set up automated alerts so relevant new postings reach you promptly rather than requiring daily manual searches.

Your digital presence functions as a persistent extension of your application materials. Ensure your LinkedIn profile is complete, current, and consistent with your resume. Use a professional photo, write a descriptive headline that communicates your professional identity, and provide detailed descriptions of your experience and accomplishments. Recruiters actively search LinkedIn for candidates, and your profile's completeness and keyword relevance decide whether you appear in their results.

Audit your broader online presence. Search for your name and review what information is publicly accessible. Employers routinely research candidates online, and content that conflicts with the professional image your application materials present can cut you from consideration. Adjust privacy settings on personal social media accounts and ensure that any publicly visible content supports rather than undermines your candidacy.

Networking as a Job Search Strategy

Networking is still the most effective job search channel. A significant proportion of positions are filled through referrals and professional connections before they are publicly posted. The networking skills covered in Chapter 33 apply directly to job searching: attend industry events, take part in professional associations, engage with alumni networks, and support relationships with contacts who work in your target fields.

Prepare a concise professional introduction that communicates who you are, what you are looking for, and what you offer. This enables contacts to find relevant opportunities and make proper introductions. Be specific about your interests and qualifications. Vague descriptions such as being open to anything make it difficult for others to help you because they cannot match your profile to specific opportunities.

Follow up consistently after networking interactions. A brief message expressing appreciation for the conversation and reinforcing your interest supports the relationship and keeps you present in the contact's awareness. When opportunities arise, people recommend individuals they remember. Consistent follow-up ensures you are remembered.

Customizing Application Materials

Tailor your resume and cover letter to each position. Review the job description carefully and align your application materials with the specific requirements, qualifications, and language used. Applicant tracking systems screen for keyword matches, and human reviewers assess relevance to the specific role. A resume that accurately reflects your qualifications but is not tailored to the position is less effective than one that explicitly connects your experience to the employer's stated needs.

Quantify accomplishments wherever possible. Specific numbers, such as percentages of improvement, dollar amounts managed, team sizes led, or project timelines met, provide concrete evidence that generic descriptions of responsibilities do not. Reviewers can evaluate specific achievements. They cannot evaluate vague claims of contribution.

Cover letters should show knowledge of the specific organization and role, explain why you are interested in this particular position, and articulate what you would contribute beyond what your resume shows. A compelling cover letter communicates that you have researched the organization and thought carefully about the fit between your capabilities and their needs.

Interview Preparation and Performance

Interview preparation begins with thorough research on the organization: its mission, products or services, recent developments, culture, and competitive position. This knowledge enables you to tailor your responses to show alignment with the organization's specific needs and values, and to ask informed questions that show genuine interest.

Prepare specific examples that show your skills and accomplishments. Behavioral interview questions ask you to describe situations where you applied particular competencies. Prepare structured responses using the situation-task-action-result format: describe the context, what you needed to conduct, what you specifically did, and what resulted from your actions. Having these examples prepared prevents the common problem of knowing you have relevant experience but being unable to articulate it clearly under interview pressure.

Prepare thoughtful questions for the interviewer. Questions about the role's specific challenges, the team's priorities, how success is measured, and the organization's development opportunities show engagement and help you evaluate whether the position is genuinely a good fit. An interview is a mutual evaluation. You are assessing the employer as much as they are assessing you.

The Road Ahead

The job search is a project that benefits from the same organizational discipline you would apply to any professional endeavor. Track applications, follow up systematically, refine your approach based on results, and support momentum through periods of slow response. Each application sent, interview conducted, and connection made develops your job search competence and brings you closer to the right opportunity. Persistence and strategic execution, not luck, are what ultimately produce results.

Chapter 37: Long-Term Career Success

Introduction

Securing a position is the beginning of career development, not its completion. Long-term professional success requires continuous skill development, deliberate relationship building, strategic reputation management, and the flexibility to adapt as industries, technologies, and personal priorities evolve. The professionals who build the most successful and satisfying careers over decades are those who treat their development as an ongoing responsibility rather than something that concluded when they were hired.

Continuous Learning and Skill Development

Industries change continuously. Technologies that define current practice become obsolete. New methodologies, tools, and knowledge appear. Professionals who stop learning after entering the workforce find their skills increasingly misaligned with market demands. Those who invest consistently in development support their relevance, expand their capabilities, and position themselves for advancement.

Continuous learning takes many forms: formal education, professional certifications, online courses, industry conferences, reading current publications in your field, and on-the-job learning through new projects and responsibilities. The specific form matters less than the consistency. Allocating regular time to development, even a few hours weekly, compounds over years into substantial ability that distinguishes you from peers who rely solely on the skills they entered with.

Seek learning opportunities that extend beyond your current role. Developing skills next to your primary ability increases your versatility and value. A technical professional who develops project management capabilities, a specialist who learns about business strategy, or a manager who gains data analysis skills becomes more valuable than someone with deeper but narrower ability. Breadth combined with depth creates professionals who can work effectively across contexts.

Take initiative in your own development rather than waiting for employers to provide training. Find the skills that will be valuable in positions you aspire to and begin developing them before you need them. Professionals who arrive at new roles with relevant skills already in development advance faster than those who begin learning only after promotion.

Building Professional Reputation

Your professional reputation is the cumulative result of your actions, reliability, quality of work, and how you treat others over time. It precedes you into every new opportunity: people will ask about you, look you up, and base first trust on what they learn from your professional history. Building a strong reputation requires no extraordinary achievement. It requires consistent competence, reliability, ethical behavior, and respectful treatment of colleagues at every level.

Deliver on commitments. Meeting deadlines, following through on promises, and producing quality work consistently are the foundation of professional credibility. People who deliver reliably earn trust, receive more responsibility, and are recommended for opportunities. People whose commitments are unreliable, regardless of their talent, find their advancement limited by the reputational cost of inconsistency.

Maintain professional relationships actively. Stay connected with former colleagues, supervisors, mentors, and professional contacts. These relationships provide referrals, recommendations, industry intelligence, and support throughout your career. Investing in relationships by offering help, sharing information, and celebrating others' achievements builds a network that provides value in both directions over time.

Manage your online professional presence deliberately. Your LinkedIn activity, published content, professional community participation, and public communications all contribute to how colleagues, recruiters, and potential collaborators perceive you. Ensure that your online presence reflects the professional identity you want to project: competent, engaged, thoughtful, and constructive.

Adaptability and Career Transitions

Few careers follow a predictable linear path. Industry disruptions, organizational changes, personal priority shifts, and unexpected opportunities create transitions that require adaptability. Professionals who treat change as a normal part of career development navigate transitions more effectively than those who expect stability and resist deviation from their original plan.

Prepare for transitions by building transferable skills and supporting a broad professional network. Technical skills specific to one industry may not transfer, but capabilities such as project management, communication, analytical thinking, leadership, and problem-solving apply across virtually every field. A diverse professional network provides information about opportunities in fields you might not otherwise discover.

When transitions occur, whether voluntary or involuntary, approach them with the same structured process you would apply to first career planning. Assess your current strengths and interests, research available options, set goals, and execute systematically. Career setbacks, including job loss, failed projects, and missed promotions, are common experiences that provide valuable information about your priorities and capabilities. How you respond to setbacks, by regrouping, learning, and moving forward, defines your career trajectory more than the setbacks themselves.

Maintain perspective on career timelines. Meaningful professional development occurs over years and decades, not weeks and months. Periods of rapid advancement alternate with periods of consolidation and learning. Comparing your progress to others' visible milestones produces anxiety without useful information, since career trajectories vary enormously based on factors both within and outside individual control. Focus on consistent development against your own goals rather than external benchmarks.

Work-Life Integration

Sustainable career success requires integration with the rest of your life. Professional achievement that comes at the cost of health, relationships, or personal wellbeing is not success in any meaningful sense. Establishing boundaries around working hours, keeping commitments outside of work, and protecting time for rest and recovery are not obstacles to professional performance but prerequisites for sustaining it.

Define what success means to you comprehensively, including professional, personal, relational, and health dimensions. Career decisions made with this broader definition in mind produce outcomes you are actually satisfied with. A promotion that requires moving away from your support network, or a higher-paying position that cuts time for activities you value, may not be genuine advancement when evaluated against your full set of priorities.

Reassess your definition of success periodically. What constitutes a fulfilling career changes as you move through different life stages, develop new interests, and refine your understanding of what matters to you. A career plan that accommodates this evolution, rather than treating your first definition as permanent, enables sustained satisfaction across decades rather than early achievement followed by growing dissatisfaction.

The Road Ahead

Long-term career success is the result of sustained effort across multiple dimensions: continuous learning, reputation building, relationship maintenance, adaptive thinking, and integration with your broader life priorities. No single decision or achievement decides your career trajectory. The accumulation of consistent, deliberate actions over years and decades produces professional lives characterized by competence, satisfaction, and meaningful contribution. Approach your career as an ongoing project that deserves the same strategic thinking and sustained attention you would give to any important endeavor.

Embracing Life Unscripted

This book addressed the practical skills and knowledge that formal education often neglects: resilience, self-care, financial literacy, digital competence, communication, and career development. Each section provided specific, actionable guidance for navigating the challenges that follow graduation, challenges that are predictable in nature even when their specific forms are not.

Knowledge alone does not produce change. Application does. The concepts and strategies presented throughout these chapters have value only to the extent that you implement them. Imperfect implementation consistently outperforms perfect understanding that is still theoretical. Start with the areas most relevant to your current circumstances, apply what you have learned, see the results, and adjust your approach based on what you discover.

The skills covered in this book are interconnected. Resilience supports career development. Financial literacy reduces stress that undermines health. Communication ability strengthens relationships that provide support during difficult periods. Self-care supports the physical and mental capacity that makes everything else possible. Improvement in any area creates positive effects across others.

Expect setbacks. Every skill described in this book develops through practice that includes failure. Financial plans meet unexpected expenses. Career plans require revision. Communication efforts sometimes fall short. Resilience is assessed precisely when circumstances are most difficult. These experiences are not evidence of inadequacy. They are the normal process through which competence develops. What matters is not whether setbacks occur but whether you respond to them by learning, adjusting, and continuing.

Your circumstances will change in ways you cannot currently predict. New challenges will arise that no book can specifically prepare you for. But the foundational capabilities addressed here, the ability to manage stress, think critically, communicate effectively, handle money responsibly, navigate technology, build relationships, and plan strategically, provide a framework that applies regardless of what specific situations you meet.

You are not starting from nothing. You bring experience, capability, and the willingness to invest in your own development that reading this book stands for. Build on that foundation deliberately. Apply what you have learned consistently. Remain open to learning from every experience, both positive and negative. The skills you develop now compound over time, producing capabilities and opportunities that are difficult to imagine from your current position but entirely achievable through sustained effort.

Your life will not follow a script. That is not a problem to solve but a reality to embrace. The most meaningful lives are built through intentional response to unscripted circumstances, through applying sound principles to unpredictable situations, and through the accumulated wisdom of experience honestly examined. You have the tools. The application is yours.

Also by David Webb

The Book On Life Unscripted
The Book On Risk Management in Payments
The Book On Strategic Obsession
The Book On High-Stakes Thinking
The Book On Artificial Leverage

About the Author

David Webb is a seasoned entrepreneur and business leader with a distinguished career spanning over three decades in the technology and services industries. As the founder and CEO of multiple successful ventures and some spectacular failures, David has shown a keen ability to drive growth, foster innovation, and lead organizations to prominence in their respective markets.

His professional journey includes founding and leading organizations that have achieved significant milestones under his guidance. David's strategic vision and leadership have been instrumental in navigating complex business landscapes and delivering value to stakeholders.

In his debut book, Life Unscripted: What You Should Have Learned in High School, David distills years of professional and personal experiences into practical insights aimed at bridging the gap between formal education and real-world application. He addresses essential life skills and knowledge areas often overlooked in traditional curricula, providing readers with the tools to navigate the complexities of adult life with confidence and competence.

About the Publisher

Welcome to The Book On Publishing

At The Book On Publishing, we believe in rewriting the rules of learning. Whether you are chasing your next big idea, building a better life, or simply curious about what should have been taught in school, you've come to the right place.

We're a platform built for dreamers, doers, and lifelong learners, offering bold, practical books and tools that empower you to take charge of your journey. From real-world skills to mindset mastery, we publish the book on what matters.

No fluff. No lectures. Just what you need to know, delivered with clarity, purpose, and a spark of curiosity.

Start exploring. Start growing. Start writing your story.

Read more at https://thebookon.ca.

Acknowledgment of AI Assistance

Portions of this book were developed with the support of AI. While every word has been carefully reviewed and refined by the author, AI served as a valuable tool for brainstorming, editing, and structuring ideas. Its aid helped accelerate the creative process and bring clarity to complex topics.

www.ingramcontent.com/pod-product-compliance
Lightning Source LLC
Chambersburg PA
CBHW051004140626
46546CB00016B/191